Until We Meet Again

Insights from the Other Side on Suicide

ANTHONY QUINATA

© 2017 Anthony Quinata
All rights reserved.

ISBN: 1546599665
ISBN 13: 9781546599661

CONTENTS

Disclaimer · v
Prologue · ix
Preface · xi
Introduction · xv

The Skeleton in Someone Else's Closet · · · · · · · · · · · · · · · · · 1
"Actually, I'm a Large." · 4
I'm Feeling Blue · 6
My Friend Teri · 12
The Unforgivable Sin? · 17
Do Those Who Commit Suicide Go to Hell? · · · · · · · · · · · 20
"If Anyone Deserves to Be in Hell…." · · · · · · · · · · · · · · · · 25
Is Suicide an Exit Plan? · 30
What's in a Name? · 32
"That's me." · 36
Diamond 'Lil, Uncle Goofy and Tor-till-las · · · · · · · · · · · · 40
The Treadmill · 43
"I'm Not Who You Think I Am." · · · · · · · · · · · · · · · · · · · 45
The Healing Place · 51
They Need Your Prayers · 55
His Inner Demons Won · 58
Mourning Has Broken · 61
It Was All I Could Do Just to Breathe · · · · · · · · · · · · · · · 67
The Lie · 69
"Life Does Kind of Make Sense." · 71
Why Me? · 77
The Reward · 80
Ask Anthony · 84
    He's Drudging Around the Other Side? · · · · · · · · · · · · 84
    What about Atheist Who Commit Suicide? · · · · · · · · · · 87

Depressed… Addicted… What Was His Life Review Like? · · · · · 88
Love Is a Two-Way Street · 90
Is He Still Angry at Me? · 91
What if Suicide is the Only Option? · · · · · · · · · · · · · · · 93
Why Shouldn't I Commit Suicide? · · · · · · · · · · · · · · · · 95
Mental Illness · 97
Is Suicide a Life Plan? · 99
Do You Really Believe That? · · · · · · · · · · · · · · · · · · · 102
Didn't She Suffer Enough? · 104
Will I See My Daughter Again? · · · · · · · · · · · · · · · · · 107
I Hurt Him… More Than I Knew · · · · · · · · · · · · · · · 109
What Do the Souls say about Assisted Suicide? · · · · · · · 111
I'm Losing the Will to Live · 113

Epilogue · 119
Acknowledgements · 125

DISCLAIMER

The information in this book is not intended to replace therapy or counseling, you are currently receiving, or may need. If you are contemplating taking your own life, or know someone who is, please let someone know. Suicidal feelings are treatable.

The author offers this material for your education, and inspiration.

The National Suicide Prevention Hotline - 1.800.273.8255.
Veteran Crisis Hotline – 1.800.273.8255 Press 1 or Text 838255

*This book is dedicated to those who know,
And those who have yet to find out.*

*And to
Saint Kateri Takakwitha,
"Lily of the Mohawks"
Canonized and Named Patron Saint of Those Who Commit Suicide
by Pope Benedict XVI
October 21, 2012*

PROLOGUE

Dearest Donna,

I'm so sorry but I was just too weak to go any further. There have been way too many things going wrong lately.

I would like you to remember that you are the best person that I ever met in this whole world. You have done more good things for me and gave me many happy times. Thank you very much.

This is <u>not</u> your fault, or anyone else's. It is nobody's fault but my own. I have no hard feelings for anybody.

Please cash this check right away. It is all I have in there. The will (will) take care of the rest.

Love,
Rene

Please take care of Christine.

June 2nd is the day my life changed forever. The person I was, I'd never be again. It's the day I lost my best friend.

Please… please… someone tell me this isn't real.

Rene, how could you leave me here? I could have helped you. I'll do anything.

God, please no! This pain hurts so much I want to die too. How can I go on without you? I can't believe you are gone.

We just talked yesterday. Why didn't you tell me? I can't believe I will never talk to you again. I'm sorry. I'm sorry I wasn't there to help you.

How can life go on?

How can people eat, laugh?

Don't they understand you are gone?

These are my thoughts the first night, the first week, the first month, the first year.

Rene and I were together for about eight years. He came into my life as a secret admirer in high school. He was two grades ahead of me. I was a Freshman; he was a Junior.

One day he walked up to me and handed me a note claiming someone asked him to give it to me. I still wish I had it. I wish I could remember what it said. It was followed by a few more notes until I finally caught onto him. From that time on we had a special friendship that turned into love.

When Rene tried to kill himself the first time he was a Senior and I was a Sophomore. The thing is, I don't really understand why he wanted to die, and why he wanted me to die with him. We didn't talk about it. He was acting strange so I called his brother and asked him to watch him. That night he was rushed to the hospital for an overdose and released a few days later.

I don't believe he received any counseling at that time. But suicide was not a real fear for me throughout the remaining time we were together, which was almost seven years. Even after we broke up, we remained best friends and were there for each other, hung out, or just called to chat which we did the day before he his suicide. He did write me a letter in which he said he was sorry and it was no one's fault but his own.

June 2nd will never be just another day for me. For the rest of my life, it will be the day Rene died.

Donna Nikolla

PREFACE

I was fast asleep, when I woke up with a start looking around the darkness of my hotel room, just a few moments before.

"Tell them it was a mistake."

I recognized the energy behind the message immediately. It was Jasmine, a young woman who crossed herself over to the hereafter on Christmas Day, 2010. The same soul who insisted that I write my first book, *Communications from the Other Side*.

I heard it again. "Tell them it was a mistake."

This time it was two voices. Jasmine's voice was joined by a male voice I didn't know.

"Tell them it was a mistake."

More voices saying the same thing.

"Tell *who* it was a mistake? What was the mistake?" I wondered.

"Tell them it was a mistake," was the only answer I received. The same message kept being repeated. Each time it was said, I heard more voices saying it until it became a cacophony.

Suddenly, they became quiet. My phone, which was on the nightstand next to the bed, dinged letting me know I'd received a Facebook message.

"My son committed suicide," The message began, "and I don't know why. Can you tell me if he's okay?"

I started to message her back when I heard a single voice this time, say, "Tell my mom I made a mistake."

■ ■ ■

There is a saying that, "Suicide is the skeleton in someone else's closet." I disagree. I believe that suicide is the skeleton in *all* our closets. I'm writing this book from the point of view of my experience as a medium, and the messages I've heard from the souls who took their own lives to their loved ones, not as a counselor or therapist.

It's been my experience, doing sessions for those who have lost someone who took their own lives, that they deal with feelings of failure, humiliation and even blame from friends and relatives. They blame themselves for not seeing any "warning signs." They often come to me hoping to hear the answer to their biggest question, *Why?*

The answer the souls often give is that they simply lost the strength, and the hope, to continue in this life. Many of these precious souls have said, in sessions that I've had the privilege of discerning, that even though they functioned in a way that allowed them to get through the day "normally," mental torture was typically a huge factor in their decision.

They've also said that once they crossed over the threshold between this life and the next, they could see what they were going through for what it really was – opportunities to grow spiritually. Their life review showed them that they did have alternatives that they didn't see, or even seemed possible, while they were still here, that would have helped them work through their issues.

God doesn't make mistakes, but understands when we do. As you'll learn, reading this book, they want to make it clear that they were not judged for what they did, nor are they condemned to "hell." Quite the opposite. They say that they're taken to a place where they can reflect, and heal, from the anguish that they thought there was no way out of.

They say that suicide is a mistake on the part of those who end their time here on earth in this way. It's a blunder they committed in the chaos they were going through. They take complete responsibility for what they've done and insist that there's nothing for you to feel guilty about.

Finally, they want you to know that you will be reunited with them on the Other Side, when you have learned the lessons you're here to learn. Until then they will continue to be with you as your "guardian angel," never abandoning you or leaving your side. They will continue doing the best they can to help you understand that everything that happens in this life benefits you in the next. Even surviving the tragedy of their suicide. They also insist that we not to see suicide as a means to speed up the reunion, or to end whatever turmoil we're experiencing.

If you're reading this book hoping to find "permission" to take your own life, thinking it's a solution to your problems, I want to make something very clear — I've never heard a soul that came through during a reading I was conducting say that this was an acceptable solution to the difficulties that we face here. According to them, you'll still need to learn on the Other Side what you didn't learn here by cutting your life short. And you must to repair the damage you leave behind.

INTRODUCTION

In the book of Genesis, chapter 1, verse 31, it says, "God saw all that He had made, and behold, it was very good." In short, life is meant to be treasured.

Beginning with the very first breath of air that enters our lungs, we learn that there is a certain sequence to life we that we can come to trust. We learn to have the confidence that the sun will rise each morning, and set every evening. We learn that while some days aren't so good, they're outnumbered by those that are. We have the expectation that we'll outlive our children, and that there will be many more days to cherish those we love. Life is good.

If, however, someone we know, someone we love, ends their life by their own hand, it's as though we're thrown into a void. In a split second, our world changes forever. We're flung into a deep hole of questions, guilt, unfinished business, and unsaid words. Perhaps worst of all, we didn't have a chance to say good-bye.

I am *not* writing this book as a psychologist, or a grief counselor. I'm a psychic medium. I have the ability, for brief periods of time, to bridge the chasm between this life and the hereafter, giving the souls of those who have crossed over a human voice. After years of doing "the work," I still see myself as a messenger, and a teacher. In my first book, *Communications from the Other Side*, I wrote about how I discovered my ability to do this, and that death is not the end of life, love, or relationships.

In my second book, *We Are Never Alone*, I shared that what the souls are constantly saying; that those we love don't leave us even though they've given up their physical bodies. They are always available when we need them.

During all the years I've been doing the work I've done more readings than I can remember in which the soul who came through who took their own life. Even so, for me, suicide was the skeleton in *their family's* closet.

Until my friend Teri did it.

"I'm supposed to be a psychic. How did I not see this coming?" I asked myself. "Did she say something and I missed it?" "Is there something I could have done to stop her from doing this?"

The idea for this book came to me one day after I kept hearing the *song, Walking on Broken Glass,* by Annie Lennox, over and over, in my head. So much so, it became an ear bug.

Later that same day, I was talking to my friend Mary on the phone and she mentioned the high number of suicides among young people where she lives in Wyoming. After I got off the phone with her, I went to a coffee shop for lunch and was talking to my friend, Marianne. I didn't talk about what Mary said, so I was surprised when, out of the blue, Marianne started talking about her father who committed suicide years before.

I mentioned this "coincidence" to another friend, Donna. She reminded me that she had also been touched by this tragedy, losing someone she loved when she was in her 20's. She told me that, 30 years later, she's still plagued by guilt and doubt.

A woman came up to my table and introduced herself as the head of the local chapter for suicide prevention. As we were talking, a police officer, who was a part of the same group walked in, along with several other people who sat on the group's board. They were there to discuss the suicide of a local police officer just two days before.

A couple of days later Donna called to tell me that someone she'd known since high school had taken his own life just that morning. That's when it occurred to me that the Eternal Light of Love, and the souls were trying to tell me something.

■ ■ ■

Whenever I do a reading for someone, I insist that I know nothing ahead of time about their loved ones they are hoping to hear from during the session. I tell them that I'm passive in the process and that they need to be open to whomever comes through during the session and what they say.

As for the souls that come through, I insist that they prove who they are. I do this by asking them questions such as, "What is your name?" "How are you related to this person?" "How did you cross over?"

Often, the attitude of the soul coming through is, "Just be quiet, and tell them what I'm telling you." I've learned over the years that I'm *not* the one in charge of what's said, or what isn't said, during a session. I'm just the messenger, and they know what their loved ones need to hear. My job is to let them know that their loved ones are okay, and provide validation that it really is the soul(s) of their loved one(s) they were hearing from.

What I can't do is take away their grief. After the session is over, survivors are typically still left with the feelings of guilt they came with.

No one teaches us what to do when this tragedy happens. Suicide survivors find themselves expected to quickly, and methodically, restructure their lives, and return to "normal." But it doesn't work that way. As one woman told me, "I was sure I was going to lose my mind".

Many of the souls I've heard from during sessions, who took their own lives, have told their loved ones that part of their journey in the hereafter is heal the hurt and confusion they caused by helping those they left behind through their grief journey. They've also talked about helping those who are still here, but not "blood related," who are dealing with the same situation(s) that they were dealing with when they were still here.

Writing this book was incredibly difficult for me. I often wrote, and rewrote sentences, even entire chapters, at the directive of the souls. It's their hope, as well the hope of the Eternal Light of Love, and my own, that this book will serve as a touchstone of stability and sanity when your world has been turned upside down. It's my hope that you start to find some semblance of healing, and peace knowing that your loved one who passed this way *is* okay, and that you will see them again.

The questions in this book are from real people. The souls are consistent, and insistent, when it comes to their answers, and they don't care how many times they must repeat what they say. Sometimes we don't hear something unless we hear it again, and again.

                              Anthony Quinata
                              May 5, 2017

THE SKELETON IN SOMEONE ELSE'S CLOSET

According to the Center for Disease Control and Prevention Data & Statistics Fatal Injury Report for 2014, each year more than 44,000 people take their own life, making it the 10th leading cause of death in America. For every person who commits suicide, there are at least 20 more who will attempt it.

Men die by suicide 3.5 times more than women.

On average, around 125 people will end their life by their own hand. *Roughly one every 13 minutes.*

Around the world, someone commits suicide *every 40 seconds.*

Suicide is the second largest cause of death worldwide among teens 15 – 19 years old.

Despite all of this, for most people, awareness of suicide comes from a far-off distance. We read about rock stars overdosing, politicians shooting themselves, and celebrities committing suicide. We hear of classmates or a casual acquaintance unexpectedly taking their own lives. Still, they all have a faraway, almost surreal quality that has little, if any, effect or impact on our own lives. We find ourselves unable to imagine being so desperate that ending our life could possibly become the only possible way out.

Thanatology, the scientific study of death and the practices associated with it, including the study of the needs of the terminally ill and their families, teaches that the ideal process of dying would be for the person to accept their imminent passing, say goodbye to their body, to their loved ones, and to life itself. It's important that the person who is dying learn to express what they're feeling, and are able to express those feelings with others, so that when the time for them to take their last breath comes, they leave this existence in peace and hope.

People are surprised when I tell them that I've done readings for people who knew they were dying and wanted to know what they could look forward to. One of those was a woman named Ann, who was dying from breast cancer. I was asked if I'd contribute a session for a silent auction being held to help pay for her medical expenses.

"I'll do one better," I said. "I'll do a reading for her." The woman who asked me for the donation of my time wasn't sure Ann would agree to it because she was an atheist, but she did.

In her reading, her aunt came through and told her that a "party" was going to be held in her honor three weeks later. "I don't know of any party except the one being held tonight," she told me.

Twenty-two days later, Ann crossed over. Ann's father, at the memorial celebrating her life, said that during the last three weeks she was alive he had never seen her happier, or more at peace. Her sister, Mary, told me that she and her parents were with Ann when she crossed over. "She told us that she wasn't afraid, and that she loved us. The last thing she said to me was, 'Are we cool?' I nodded yes. She closed her eyes, and stopped breathing."

As I mentioned before, that's supposed to be the ideal way we lose a loved one to death.

Those whose loved ones take their own lives aren't typically given this opportunity. For them, the illusion of, "That happens to other families, not normal families like mine," is shattered. Suddenly, the world isn't as safe as you thought it was, and you're afraid - very afraid; and understandably so.

As if that weren't bad enough, the chances of a someone else in the family taking their own life goes up 400%.

A loved one who kills themselves does so in a desperate attempt to end their own pain; but for those left behind, the anguish isn't over – it's only passed on. They find themselves struggling to put the pieces of their lives back together, while dealing with guilt, shame, blame and unanswered questions, such as, "Why did they do it?"

"What did I miss?"

"Is there something I could have done to stop it?"

Sometimes they come to someone like me, a psychic medium, for answers.

"ACTUALLY, I'M A LARGE."

I was born on Guam, to parents who were both from Guam, an island in the Western Pacific that I like to say is so Catholic, it hurts. It's a Guamanian custom, when someone dies, we say a novena (9 days of prayers) for the repose of their soul. On the 9th day, we bury them, and throw a *huge* party celebrating their entrance in Heaven.

After that, we never talk about them again. It's believed that doing so disturbs their peace.

This is the culture I was raised in, so when my book, "Communications from the Other Side," came out talking about being a "medium," a friend of mine who is also Guamanian, said to me, "You not only lost your Church, you lost your entire culture."

What I'm trying to say is that it was never *my* idea to do this work. I believe that the work chose me.

Like most people, I wondered what happened after we died. I didn't know what a "medium" was, or that they claimed to be able to communicate with those who have passed on. I still remember the day I was in the parking lot of a shopping center, weeping, praying, telling God that if life didn't continue after death, I didn't get it —

Why do we fall in love?
Why do we suffer?
What was the point of it all?

Back in the '80's, when I lived in Salt Lake City, Utah, I met a man who was in his 70's. Both he and his wife were avowed atheists. One day I saw him leaving his apartment and asked, "Going for a walk?"

"Yeah… trying to hold on to this precious thing we call 'life' for as long as I can," he told me.

"Why? If there's nothing after this, you'll never know you were here to begin with." I wasn't trying to challenge him. I honestly wanted to hear what he had to say. He didn't answer me, but just kept walking.

Several years later when my friend Sarah died in a tragic accident, I didn't know what to think. As I was on my way to her memorial service, being Catholic, and a paranormal investigator at the time, I believed that she not only had survived death, but could even hear me when I talked to her. I just didn't think she could talk to me. So, when I told her how much I appreciated who she was, our friendship, and how much I'd miss her, I came close to having to have to change my underwear when I "heard" her speaking back to me.

"I love you too, Anthony," I heard. It wasn't a voice, more like a thought. Which I why I thought what I was hearing was simply my mind expressing my grief. "I loved our friendship, and I'll miss you too, until we meet again. By the way, tell my family that I'm okay, will you?"

It was that last sentence that made me almost run into the back of a parked car. It was also what made me wonder if I really had heard from Sarah. After all, why would I even think such a thing?

I couldn't bring myself to tell Sarah's husband or parents what she asked me to, but that "conversation" *is* what started me on the path to discovering I had the ability to connect those who have passed away with their loved ones still here. (Although if you would have asked me at the time if I thought I was a medium, I would have said, "No… I'm a large!)

I'M FEELING BLUE

I used to do group sessions with up to 12 people at a time at Cornerstone Books, in Englewood, Colorado. One night, I was joined by filmmakers, Rachel Perry and Miguel Tarango. They were there to video the session that night as part of a documentary they wanted to make about me and what I do.

The way my group sessions worked back then was if you were interested in getting a reading, you simply showed up the night of the session, and paid your fee to attend. You didn't have to sign up ahead of time. You didn't have to give your name at the door, and you were prohibited from speaking to anyone about whom you were hoping to hear from. I wanted to ensure that everyone who showed up received a reading, which is why attendance in the group was limited to no more than twelve people at a time.

I explained all of this to Rachel and Miguel while we were eating dinner before going to the store. Which is why Rachel was surprised when, 30 minutes before anyone arrived in the parking lot, I told her, "Someone is coming to hear from a loved one who took their own life."

"How do you know?" she asked.

"Because I can feel the energy of the soul who did it, and it's as heavy as it gets." Doing "the work" can be exhausting and draining, both for me, and the souls who choose to communicate with their loved ones using me as their messenger.

To be able to "hear" what the souls want to say, and then give them a human voice, I must raise my energy. Think of it as me turning a ceiling fan up to high speed when I'm working. At the same time, I also go into a state of mind I can only compare to as "daydreaming," which is why I end up forgetting what the messages are that were passed along as soon as the session ends. Kind of like forgetting a dream as soon as you wake up.

It's exhausting for the souls because for them to communicate, they must *lower* their energy. Worse still, they must rely on a fragile and faulty instrument, my brain, to convey their messages. To make matters even worse, *anyone* who knows me personally will tell you that I sometimes have a hard time understanding the person standing right next to me.

I like to joke that one time, during a reading, a woman who was coming through told me that she had "acute angina." I told her husband that she was saying she had "a cute …." Never mind.

The souls use several ways to get their messages across, but it's not like I'm having a conversation with them. As I mentioned before, the messages typically come across as a thought, feeling, or emotion. How do I know it's coming from the Other Side? Because I typically don't think things like, "I died from breast cancer."

Another way a soul might get this message across is to show me symbols. A pink ribbon may mean they passed from breast cancer, survived it, or were involved in the fight against that horrible disease. If they died in their sleep, or in a coma, because I'm Catholic, they'll show me Saint Joseph, the "patron saint" of a peaceful death. If the passing was recent, I'll see Saint Anthony, the Church's patron saint of things lost. If someone prays constantly and continually, I'll see rosary beads. They show me these things because of my Catholic upbringing, even if the person I'm doing the session for isn't, because they know it's a way that I can relate to.

Sometimes, what I see seems "Catholic," but has nothing to do with the religion. I once told a woman whose son committed suicide that Mary, the mother of Jesus, was praying for her.

"Why would she be praying for *me?*" I was asked. "I'm not Catholic!"

"Neither is she," I laughed, "but she is a mother, and she knows what it feels like to lose a child."

Sometimes I'll see Jesus carrying a cross during a session, especially with someone who committed suicide because of the suffering the person went through, the heavy burden they carried, before they killed themselves.

Beyond that, a symbol could mean many things, and it's up to me to figure what it means. Over the years and through countless sessions, I've learned that if I see a lit candle it could be an acknowledgement of prayers being said for that soul, or it could be a request for prayers. The soul may even be asking that a candle be lit for them.

If I'm being shown a car accident it may mean that the soul crossed over due to a car accident, that the passing was accidental, or that the person sitting in front of me was in a car accident.

If I smell that "new car" smell, it could mean that the sitter just bought a new car, or that their car was just repaired, or needs to be repaired.

If someone passed from COPD, lung cancer, or emphysema, my lungs will feel heavy. I'll feel all the symptoms of a heart attack if that's how the soul coming through passed. If it's from a long-term illness, I'll feel myself become weaker and weaker, until the sitter acknowledges this.

If someone lost their lives at the hands of another by being shot, I'll feel the impact of the bullet. If they were stabbed, I'll feel as though I'm being stabbed. Once when a man was coming through who was beaten to death, I felt as though I were being hit all over my head, chest and stomach area to the point I wanted to collapse onto the floor.

A metallic taste in my mouth may mean that someone had cancer and went through chemotherapy, or that they put a gun in their mouth and pulled the trigger.

Seeing "Tiny Tim" the singer from the '60's best known for the song, "Tiptoe Through the Tulips," tells me that what I'm about to bring up is potentially very upsetting for the person receiving the messages.

A birthday cake means I'm supposed to acknowledge a birthday coming up, or just passed, for an adult. A wrapped present means it's for a child.

I could go on but the point I'm trying to make is that I'm nothing more than the instrument in the process as far as the souls are concerned. They really don't care if what they're trying to communicate makes sense to me or not, because it's not supposed to. What they care about is that it makes sense to the person receiving the messages.

Sometimes the sitter won't understand because the messages aren't meant for the person receiving them. Or I may be right but the sitter isn't understanding what's being said, for whatever reason. I encourage people to record the sessions for this reason because it's not unusual for things to make sense later.

I once did a session for a man whose young son had a disease which would take his life at a very young age. He came to me while his son was still alive because he was a forensic psychiatrist and was hoping that I would convince him that life really did continue after we pass away. During the session, his grandfather came through.

"Your grandfather is asking me to tell you to let your mother know that your sister is with him, and that he's taking good care of her."

"I don't have a sister," he responded. I could sense that his skepticism *immediately* turned into cynicism.

"Did I misunderstand something?" I wondered. But no, his grandfather repeated what he said, and so I repeated it as well.

"I *don't* have a sister."

"Did your mother miscarry, or terminate a pregnancy?" I asked him.

"No. If she did, I would have known about it." He walked away from the session feeling it had been a complete waste of his time.

Three years later I received a message from him on Facebook, reminding me who he was and how I told him what his grandfather had said. "I wanted to tell you that I was talking to my mother today, and she told me that she did have a miscarriage before she had me. It was a girl. I thought you might like to know. I'm sorry I was such a douche bag to you that night."

Another time, I did a telephone session for two sisters, one of whom lost her son to suicide. I told them, "When I ask him about his passing, he points at himself. To me that means that he's taking responsibility for his death. Does that make sense?"

"Yes."

"He's drawing the letter 'M' and showing me Saint Michael. Do you take the name Michael, living or deceased?"

"That's my son's name... Michael."

Even though Michael took his own life, he was at a point in his journey on the hereafter that he came across as fun loving and full of energy. He shared stories that made his mother, aunt, and me, laugh. "He's telling me he stole a car. Do you understand this?"

"No."

"When I say he 'stole' a car, I mean he drove it without permission. That's the way he's talking about it. He's making me feel as though the car he drove didn't belong to him. It might have even been yours!"

That's when his mother remembered that when Michael was three years old, he took car keys off a table, climbed into her car, somehow managed to put it in gear, sending it forward, crashing into the side of the house.

Later, as the session was coming to an end I saw blue... lots of blue. I could see different shades of blue... from light to dark. I also saw a blue bracelet with Michael's name on it. I mentioned this and asked if "blue" Michael's favorite color.

"No."

"Did someone paint a bedroom blue? He's now showing me blue paint, and making me feel like someone's room was painted blue."

"No."

"Is there something, anything, in the room you two are in that's blue?"

"No."

I was confused and decided to let it drop as Michael was pulling his energy away, ending the session.

Ten minutes after we hung up, they sent me a picture on my phone of a blue bong, with different shades of blue painted on it, and a blue bracelet with the name Michael sitting on the bowl. They admitted that as the session was going on they were smoking marijuana... using the blue bong. It never occurred to them that this is what Michael was talking about.

For Michael, it was his way of letting them know he was with them at *that* moment.

As I looked at the picture I imagined the two of them passing the bong back and forth, during the reading, saying to one another, "Blue? I don't see anything blue. Do you?"

"Nope." Flick... bubble... inhale.

The next day Michael's mother was telling his sister about the reading and the blue bong, and how I asked if someone painted their room blue. "Mom," his sister said, "the day after Michael's funeral, dad painted Michael's room blue."

Flick... bubble... inhale.

MY FRIEND TERI

Teri and I met when we were both staying in the same extended stay hotel. The first time I saw her she was standing at the front desk, talking and laughing with whomever was working the desk that night.

As we became friends, I found out that dancing was one of her passions. She had two other loves Clifford and Paco, her two dogs. A few months later, she adopted a third fur baby. "The moment I saw him I knew his name was supposed to be Bentley," she told me. He looked like a Miniature Pinscher, and had the energy of a Jack Russell. His body was muscular, and his eyes bright. He really was, and is, a good-looking dog, and the name fit him perfectly.

A month or so later, I adopted Bentley's brother from the same litter. He originally went to a woman who also lived in the hotel, on the same floor as Teri. The woman named him, "Justice." Like Bentley, he had a great deal of puppy energy, and she quickly decided he was too much for her to handle. A couple on the second floor took him in. It only took a couple of weeks for them to decide the same thing. They asked me if I would take him. I agreed.

"Don't worry, Justice. You've just found your forever home," I told him. I didn't care for his name, and since this was his third chance at finding a home, and he was giving me a chance to love and take care of him, I named him, "Chance," as a reminder of how lucky we both were.

It didn't take me long to find out that Chance had *a lot* of energy. Even more than Bentley. I started referring to him as my "weapon of mass destruction," and had to walk him often. I thought it might help if I had him run on the hotel's treadmill, but even after doing that for 30 minutes, he'd jump off and still want to go for a walk!

"I should have named you '5 Miles,'" I told him. "That way I can tell people, 'I walked 5 Miles today.'" Which is probably how far we did walk on a typical day.

I lived on the first floor, and Teri told me that whenever she walked her dogs by my room, Bentley seemed to know which room Chance and I were in, and would often look at the window of my room and cry as they walked by. So, we made plans for a "play date" for the two brothers to get together. Unfortunately, between her schedule and mine, it never happened.

One afternoon I was standing at the front desk talking to the woman behind the counter when Teri walked up, and announced, "Guess what! It's my birthday today! Since I have no one to celebrate it with me, I guess you two (the front desk clerk and I) will have to do!" she laughed.

I was stunned by what she said because I knew she had a lot of friends, as well as family in the area. "I'll tell you what," I told her. "I was just about to head out to one of the restaurants nearby for dinner. Why don't you join me?" I don't remember why, but that didn't happen either.

Two weeks later, I saw her again. "What kind of leash do you use for Chance?" Teri asked. It looked to me as though Bentley had a growth spurt, "It's like he's on steroids or something," she told me. She said he had broken two leashes in the past couple month. Chance was a bit bigger and three pounds heavier. Like Bentley, he was all muscle. So, I told her about the nylon leash I used.

"If Bentley ever becomes too much for you, let me know, and I'll be happy to take him," I offered.

"No way!" she said. "I couldn't do that! I don't know how people can have a dog for a year, and give them up like that!"

"Well, I didn't mean to upset you. I was just thinking that since I have his brother...."

I didn't see her again for another week. Even though it was late in the day, and dark, I knew it was her because she was wearing one of her signature "Hello Kitty" hats. I was taking Chance for a walk, and Teri was walking through the parking lot of the hotel. I could tell from her body language that she was upset. She looked at me, and didn't say anything. I wondered if she was upset with me about my offer to take Bentley, so I started to follow her but by the time Chance and I got to the lobby, she was already in the elevator, and the door was closing.

The following night, another guest saw her at the vending machines on the floor she lived on. He said that she was happy, smiling, and laughing. "She was on top of the world." Whatever she was upset about the night before was apparently a distant memory.

The next day, she didn't come down to the front desk, which was odd. She followed the same routine every week. Every Friday, she'd remind come to remind the person at the front desk that she'd pay her rent after Fed Ex delivered her check. Then she'd come back on Saturday and drop off money.

When she didn't show up the day after that, the hotel staff knew something was wrong. On Sunday, Christine, the assistant manager tried calling her to see if she was okay. She didn't answer her phone. Christine called Chris, the head of maintenance, and they went to her room.

When Teri didn't come to the door, Christine, afraid that something might be wrong, used her master key to open the door, and called her name. The door's security latch kept the door from opening completely. Chris got a bolt cutter.

He went into the room first. Bentley was in the kitchen barking at him. Paco was on the bed, next to his mother, barking as well. Clifford was nowhere to be seen. Teri laying on the bed, her dark skin "as white as the sheet she was laying on." Turning around and blocking Christine from seeing what he just saw, he told her, "Call the police."

I didn't know that any of this was going on. I found out when I went up to the third floor to go to Chris's room to see if he'd like to join me for dinner, since it was his day off. As I was getting on the elevator an Animal

Control officer was coming out of it. I didn't think anything of it because many of the guests of the hotel had pets.

As I passed Teri's room, I noticed something on her door from Animal Control. I stopped and read it, wondering if something happened with one of her dogs. The notice said that if she didn't pick them up in 7 days they would be turned over to the county. I thought of the officer I just saw leaving the hotel, and hurried down the stairs hoping to catch up with her. Luckily, she was still in the parking lot filling out paperwork.

"Hi. I was walking by my friend's room when I saw your notice on her door. Are her dogs okay?"

"They're in the back of my truck," she answered.

"Are they okay?" I asked again.

"They're alright," she answered me, "but she won't be picking them up."

"What do you mean? Is *she* okay?" I asked. "There's no way she wouldn't come for her babies," I thought to myself. I started to panic wondering if Teri was in the hospital.

"She's deceased," the officer said quietly.

I couldn't believe what I was hearing. "What?"

"She deceased," the officer repeated.

I immediately became concerned for Clifford, Paco and Bentley, and asked what would happen to them. The officer explained that they would offered to Teri's family first. I felt relieved to hear that. I told her that I had Bentley's brother. She asked me which one was Bentley, and I described him. "He's in the back of the truck; right behind me," she told me.

I looked and the only one I could see was Bentley, who was looking back at me, obviously terrified. I called out to Clifford and Paco, as well, telling them that I would make sure they're all okay. The officer wrote out a case number on one of her cards.

I took the card and went back into the hotel. Instead of taking the elevator, I ran up the stairs to the third floor, and stood in front of the door to Teri's room. As I just stood there, the officer's words, 'She won't be picking up the dogs. She's deceased,' kept ringing in my ears. I could hear two police officers quietly talking to each other on the other side of the door. I wanted to knock and ask them what happened to my friend.

A moment later, I knew what happened. I could feel an impact to my chest. The area of my heart to be exact. I knew at that moment she was shot in the heart. I didn't find out until later that she had done it to herself.

A few days later Teri's mother and sister came to the hotel to get Teri's personal belongings. They told the staff that they picked Clifford, Paco, and Bentley up from the shelter they were in. One of the housekeepers told them that I had Bentley's brother and that I had expressed an interest in taking him.

Clifford went to one of Teri's cousins. Paco was with Teri's mom. Even though Bentley didn't seem to trust men, they said they would see how he reacted to me.

A few days later, Teri's mother, her sister, and one of her cousins came to the hotel with Bentley. We were all surprised when he saw me and wanted me to pick him up.

After Teri's memorial service, her mother and sister went through her room again to pick up some more of her things. Her mother told the manager to give me permission to go into Teri's room afterwards to get what I needed for Bentley.

While I was in there, Craig, one of the hotel's maintenance staff, was there as well. I was putting Bentley's things in a box, along with a few personal things that belonged to Teri so that Bentley would always have something to help him remember his mommy.

"It's too bad Teri did what she did," Craig said quietly. "Now she won't be able to enter into the kingdom of Heaven."

"Oh, I don't know about that," was all I said, as I picked up the box.

"You don't?" he asked, looking at me, sounding surprised.

"No, I don't," I answered, and walked out the door.

THE UNFORGIVABLE SIN?

Many years ago, I was a young mom and one of the adult youth group leaders in my church. It was a large Christian, nondenominational church in the south, but not much different than the Baptist churches I grew up attending. The youth group was growing fast.

Jacob was one of those kids that stood out from the rest. Adults liked to hang out with him. He was charismatic, funny, intelligent, talented, and wise beyond his years. Whenever the church had a play or production involving the youth, the bigger roles were given to Jacob because he always played them perfectly. He was a natural-born star, and had the perfect balance of confidence and humbleness. He was kind to others and a great friend to many of the other kids in the youth group. He had a huge heart for ministry and worked hard to make friends with kids who didn't fit in. He refused to wear brand-named clothes. He'd pick out the craziest outfits he could find at the local thrift store and wear them to school. He'd get made fun of from time to time but he seemed to let it roll off his back as he smiled.

He had wonderful parents. They were young when they had him and they were very involved in church and the youth group as well. They were very understanding, humble, and kind people. Jacob's dad taught him to play several different instruments and they often played music together. They had a great relationship. I'm sure things weren't perfect but there were no signs of the family being anything other than a loving, close family that worked through their problems together. Jacob had two younger siblings and he was very sweet and protective towards them.

Youth pastors started rotating through the church over the next few years and youth group members and helpers became discouraged and slowly scattered in different directions. I lost touch with most of them for a year or two. One day I heard that Jacob had just graduated high school, had a steady girlfriend, and then found out she was pregnant. It was rumored that he suddenly wasn't handling life so well. I figured he was just slow to go through his teenage rebellion phase and it finally had hit. I was sure in a few more years I'd hear about how he had overcome all of that and was on the verge of ruling the world. However, a few months later, I ran into him at the restaurant he worked at. I was so happy to see him all grown up and looking happy. I was so proud of him even though I had nothing to do with it. I hated that I didn't have but a few moments to speak as I was rushed through the buffet line of hungry people.

"Hi Jacob! How have you been?" I said.

He beamed a huge smile back at me and proudly said, "Did you hear I'm going to be a daddy?!"

"Yes, I did! You are going to be the best daddy ever!" I answered, almost tearing up. Those were the last words I ever got to say to him.

A week later, his mother was calling everyone she'd ever known, frantically searching for her son. They had a big argument and he left the house and never came back. He was found the next day in his car in a wooded area.

It was the most awful funeral I'd ever been to. Hundreds of people crowded into a big church and loudly sobbed uncontrollably for hours. His poor mother clung to his casket begging him over and over to come back to her. His father was clinging to his wife, trying to hold it all together and not knowing what to do. Jacob's two younger siblings sat on the front pew with their heads hung low, never looking up. The amount of suffering they all went through and still go through is unimaginable.

I went back to the church youth group to visit the ones that were still there. We all sat around and cried and talked it out. Why would God allow this to happen? We were angry and we didn't even know what exactly we were angry at. We were angry with ourselves for not knowing he needed help and not saying something or doing something to prevent it. We all wished he had given us a clue that he was going to end his own life. We all second-guessed our own judgment and wondered if he had given clues that we missed. How many other people around us are contemplating suicide and we don't know it? We were upset that his family had to go through this and we couldn't do anything to help them. Words seemed so meaningless.

Some were angry at Jacob for doing it. Some were angry that God allowed it to happen. We talked about how we had been taught that those who kill themselves are committing the ultimate unforgivable sin. We wondered if Jacob was in hell. We couldn't fathom that God would send such a wonderful soul like Jacob to hell. If He could not forgive Jacob, then why would He ever forgive us for our sins?

Andi Graham

DO THOSE WHO COMMIT SUICIDE GO TO HELL?

Wrestling with, and always wondering about the whys, and imagining the what-ifs, people who lose a loved one to suicide come to me with questions.

A woman named Robin wrote to me, "My son killed himself. People keep telling me my child's in hell. I don't know but it that's true, then that's where I belong to."

Speaking as a psychic medium who has helped connect many souls who have taken their own lives with loved ones they left behind, I was able to tell her, "No, it's *not* true."

In fact, according to the souls, "hell" doesn't exist. At least, not on the Other Side. So where did this idea come from?

It might surprise you to find out that the word "hell" has its origins in real estate! "Hell" is an old English word for a corral used to keep animals contained. If you wanted to confine a cow or pig, you would "hell" it in by building an enclosure. There was nothing blasphemous or religious about the word.

Hell, for those who commit suicide existed *before* they took their life, not after. Since n*othing* is beyond the understanding and wisdom of the Beautiful One, no soul is punished for ending their own life.

Along with beating themselves up about not having seen the "warning signs," there's also the big question of, "Why?" People come to me hoping to hear from their loved one the reason why their father shot himself, their mother took so many pills, or their child hung themselves.

The answer, from all the souls I've heard from during these sessions, can be summed as, "I simply lost all of my strength to continue living. I didn't want to die. I didn't want to hurt you. I just wanted the pain to end."

"Do they know how much I'm hurting and how much I miss them?"

"Do they regret what they did?"

These are two of the many questions that often come up during these readings. The answer to these and similar questions is, "Yes." During their "life review," they are shown the impact of what they did on the lives of their loved ones. And it's up to them to determine what they need to do from where they are in the hereafter to try to ease the turmoil their passing created, and help their loved ones put one foot in front of the other as they move forward in their journey through their grief.

Given what the souls say, I wonder why so many religions have taken such a hardline stance against it. Then again, it's not as though any religious leaders have asked me.

People typically assume it's because the scriptures of various religions, especially Judaism and Christianity, condemn it, but the truth is that it's just not the case. If you read the Bible very carefully, you will not find any clear disapproval or ban of taking one's own life anywhere. It may even surprise you to know that the Biblical attitude toward suicide ranges from thoughtfulness to praise.

I found five examples of suicide in the Bible (there are more) – in the book of 2 Samuel, 17:23, the prophet Achitophel hung himself after betraying David. Zimri burned down his house, with him in it, after a military defeat in 1Kings 16:18. The suicide of Saul in 1Samuel and 1Chronicles. Samson in Judges 16:28. And finally, Judas, the disciple who betrayed Jesus in Matthew 27:3-5.

Pope Tertullian (155-245 A.D.) considered Jesus' death a form of suicide in that he (Jesus) had chosen to die the way he did. Suicide, in Tertullian's time, was so common that no one paid much attention to it when it happened. Only slaves and soldiers, who were considered property, were denied the right to kill themselves.

There is nothing in any of these stories that condemns the suicides. Not only that, but I couldn't find anything in either Jewish nor Christian scriptures prohibiting suicide. In fact, Judas' suicide was praised as being the right thing to do, an attitude shared by many Christians today.

Other cultures admired people who knowingly went to their deaths, such as the Vikings, Druids, many African tribes, Eskimos, and the Japanese. Early Greek literature is filled with examples of people who nobly took their own lives. The Aegean Sea was named after Aegeus, King of Athens, father of the hero Theseus, after he threw himself in the sea.

What changed?

During the Sixth Century, Saint Augustine (354 – 430 A.D.), a Catholic Bishop and theologian, argued that Christianity was founded on the belief that the human body contained the soul, and that life is a gift from God. In the Book of Genesis, 1:31 it says that, "God saw all that He had made, and behold, it was very good." In other words, life is good, and a gift from God. Rejecting life means rejecting God. Killing oneself, being made in God's image and likeness, is equivalent to killing God. Due to Augustine's writings, the Catholic Church declared that the consequence of suicide was "eternal damnation."

In the year 533 A.D. the Council of Orleans decided that those who committed suicide were to be denied funeral rites.

In 693 A.D., the Church ruled that attempting suicide was grounds for excommunication.

The bodies of those who committed suicide were to be taken to a place of disgrace, where it was put on display. The body was hung on a frame, and could not be taken down without permission from the local judge.

When the body was finally allowed to be taken down, it was usually buried at a crossroads, and a stone placed over its face. The purpose of this was so that its soul would never find its way to heaven.

Suicide victims and their families, were ostracized, shamed, and legally punished. At one time in England, suicide was considered a crime against the king because it deprived the ruler of taxes. The victim was not permitted burial in a church cemetery, and the family's property was confiscated so that the king could be reimbursed for his loss.

To this day, beliefs that make suicide, and those who take their own life an abomination before God still endure, and yet, suicides continue.

Melanie was 19 years old when she told her roommate that she was going to drive to Las Vegas to watch her brother, a recording artist and bona fide rock star, perform in a concert. Sometime later her roommate smelled a strange odor. She opened the door leading to the garage, and exhaust fumes came billowing into the house. Melanie was still in her car.

During the reading with her parents I asked, "Are you Catholic?"

"No."

"The reason I ask is that she's showing me a crucifix on a chain. She says she was wearing it when she passed."

"She was wearing a crucifix, which struck us as strange. We're Presbyterian," I was told.

I sat quietly for a moment listening to the young soul explain why she wore the cross of Catholicism. "She's telling me that she put it on hoping that God wouldn't forget her when she died. She wants you to know that she finally found the peace there that she couldn't find here."

Even though the souls insist that *no one* has the "right" to take their own life, they also assert, without exception, that they are safely in the arms of the Beautiful One, and that whatever anguish drove them to end their own life, is over. They are at peace, with God, with themselves, and with what they had done. While you and I may experience things in our life that make us wonder how much more we can endure, we develop a shell that we can protect ourselves with until the pain passes, we overcome whatever obstacles are in front of us, or we learn the lesson that the suffering we had to endure is revealed to us. These precious souls could not, for whatever reason, develop the safeguards they needed to do the same, and they lost the strength, and desire, to continue going on in this life.

Thankfully, the Eternal Light of Love understands this.

Despite her fears, God didn't forget, or reject, Melanie or anyone else who loses the will to fight anymore. They aren't in "hell," but are held, enfolded, and embraced in unconditional love, helping them to heal the hurt and confusion they were going through, and the consequences of what they've done.

"IF ANYONE DESERVES TO BE IN HELL...."

Shortly after my book, *Communications from the Other Side,* came out I received a call from my friend, Gina. A friend of hers committed suicide but not before he killed his girlfriend. She contacted me after receiving a "reading" from another friend who claimed to be a medium. During her session, Gina started crying.

"Why are you crying for him?" her friend asked. "He's in hell where he belongs."

Gina asked me if I thought what she said was true.

"First," I answered her, "how much did you pay her for this reading?"

"Nothing."

"Good, because that's *exactly* how much it was worth."

■ ■ ■

Several months *before* my book came out, I was on the East Coast, doing seminars and small group sessions. One of the sponsors of the events thought it would be fun to go on a "cemetery ghost tour." I agreed to go, but only because the guide said that I wouldn't have to pay the tour fee. It didn't take me long to become bored with the whole thing so I went off on my own.

I eventually found myself in front of four grave stones. There was a man's marker on the left, a woman's on the right, with two children in between them. Across the road, to the left, was another marker with a woman's name and a picture of a child in front of it in a plastic sleeve.

When the tour caught up with me, I couldn't tell them why I was drawn to this area, or to the markers I was standing in front of. I did say to them that I felt that the marker of the woman with the photo in front of it was somehow connected to them though. Before I walked I away I said a silent prayer - "I'm here to reconnect people with their loved ones who have crossed over. If there's anyone you want to speak to through me, please inspire them to come to one of my events."

The following Thursday I was doing a small group session for about 11 people. I went around the room giving messages to everyone there. That's how a woman named Brenda heard from her son.

"Do you take the name Brian, living or deceased?"

"Yes."

"Deceased."

"Yes."

"Okay, because he keeps insisting that I tell you that he's okay. He's coming across very loudly, and strong. He wants me to tell you… he wants you to know he's not being punished by God, for what he did, but he has a lot of work to do repairing the damage he caused. Do you know what he means?"

"Yes," she said, obviously relieved to hear what I just told her. Tears were streaming down her face.

"Do you take the name Lisa?"

"Yes."

"Living?"

"Yes."

"His sister?"

"Yes."

"He has another sister. Passed."

"Yes."

"Okay. I wasn't sure but it explains why he's calling out to Lisa, but saying to me at the same time, 'She's not the sister who's here with me.' Please tell her you heard from her brother."

"I will."

"He thanks you and her for what you're both doing since he's been gone. Do you understand this?"

"Yes."

After a few more messages were relayed he started to pull his energy away. "He keeps insisting that I let you know that he's okay. He's busy on the Other Side making up for what he did, but he's okay."

The next day, Brenda called the woman who organized the session and asked for my phone number. When she got a hold of me she wanted to know if she could arrange a private session with her and her daughter before I left.

"I called my daughter that night and told her I heard from Brian. She kept calling me back wanting to know what was said. Was he okay? Did I really think it was him? Can she talk to him too? She kept calling me until four in the morning!"

We agreed to meet the following morning.

When I saw them, Brenda looked bright and hopeful, but Lisa's face was tight. I could tell she wasn't sure that I really was able to hear from her brother. I knew from my conversation with Brenda on the phone that she and Lisa were hoping to hear from Brian again, but sitting there in front of them I told them I couldn't promise anything. That they had to be open to *whomever* came through.

"We said a prayer on our way over here asking him to and talk to us."

"Good!" I exclaimed. "That always helps. In fact, God, and Brian have answered your prayers; Brian's here," I told them. They both began crying. As soon as I started passing on what I was hearing, I could tell that that they both knew it really was him.

What happened next literally took my breath away. Brian's wife showed up. She wanted them to know that she and Brian were together in the hereafter. So were two of their three children.

Two of their three children?

Why did this sound familiar?

That's when it hit me. These were two of the four souls whose markers I was standing in front of at the cemetery that were coming through. It took my breath away, and I had to pause to let the reality of what was happening sink in – for me.

His wife talked about being separated from Brian and seeing someone else. One night, Brian had the kids for an overnight visit. She was going to pick them up and take them to a children's themed restaurant for the afternoon. She wrote on Facebook before she went to pick them up that she hoped it would be a good day. That was the last thing she wrote. Brian shot her, then their children, before killing himself. One of the children survived.

Suddenly, another soul showed up. Someone saying that she was Brenda's daughter; Lisa's sister. A week after the tragedy involving her brother, his wife and children, she took her own life as well. Her marker was the one to the left with the picture on it. When I told Brenda and Lisa this they nodded their head. Brenda told me that she had taken her daughter's child into her home.

Her daughter wanted them to know that she was with her brother, his wife, their children, and God, whom the souls often refer to as, "The Eternal Light of Love." She and her brother were working on healing the pain that they endured while they were here, and that their passing caused.

I want to admit two things to you as I finish this story. First, when I heard what Brian had done, I thought to myself, "If *anyone* belongs in Hell, it's this guy." I'm embarrassed, even ashamed to admit it, but it's the way I felt.

Secondly, I was angry that this guy seemed to be getting away with what he did. I even started crying during the session when I heard this, something the souls have told me is a no-no. I'm only the messenger. I'm not to judge what I hear. I'm not to get involved. It's really none of my business.

"Besides," Brian's wife chastised me," it's not like he's getting away with anything. God's law demands that he comes to terms with what he did, and repair the damage that he caused. That is a form of hell in, and of, itself."

Lisa and I became friends after the session ended. She often told me how much it helped her to hear from them, and to know that her brother was all right where he was. She was happy he was with his wife and kids.

I recently found out that Lisa is now with her sister and brother in the hereafter. I know that she is happy with to be reunited with her brother, sister, and sister in law, as they watch over her Brenda and the children until they're together again.

I'll miss you, Lisa, until we meet again, on the Other Side.

IS SUICIDE AN EXIT PLAN?

Not according the souls I've heard from. We come here for a specific purpose, a lesson we need to learn, along with a plan to fulfill that purpose and learn that lesson. Once we've achieved that, learning all that we came here to learn, and teaching all that we came here to teach, the time comes for us to return home to the Other Side. *Not until then.*

Of course, all that changes when someone commits suicide. Which has led some people to ask me, "Is it possible that suicide is the exit plan chosen by someone before they came here?"

I've heard of people who claim to be mediums saying that people who cross themselves over do so because it was part of their life plan *before* they came here.

I've never discerned a single soul that recommended suicide to get to achieve the peace, love and tranquility experienced on the Other Side. Not even from those who committed suicide themselves. What they do say is that they could have accomplished more by working out their problems while they were still here. They insist that what they did was like dropping out of school. Any lessons they came here to learn on earth that were cut short *must* be continued where they are. There's no way around it. There are no shortcuts. And because there's no one who gets in your face for what you did, learning those lessons is more difficult on the Other Side.

People have become upset with me when I tell them this, because it's one way they've rationalized to themselves what happened. Their loved one came into this life knowing that's the way they were going to leave it. But no matter what others have said, the souls I've heard from say it's just not true. We come here to fulfill a unique purpose in this life that only we can accomplish. We come here to learn, and teach, lessons of love and compassion in the face of the difficulties we all encounter, not to inflict the sort of pain suicide often leaves in its wake.

When someone takes their own life they must acknowledge, on the Other Side, the chaos they leave behind, and they need to do what they can, from there, to ease the turmoil. Every time I hear a "medium" claiming that someone took their own life because it was part of their life plan, I think to myself, "Are you kidding? Don't they realize that what they're implying is that someone came here planning to create that kind of havoc? That hardly sounds like what the souls say is the purpose we all share of 'recreating heaven here on earth' to me."

Which leads to my whole point. It's not something that they ever envisioned before they came here.

WHAT'S IN A NAME?

Being nosey is an asset when it comes to being a medium. Even though I'm passive during a reading allowing the souls to tell me what they know their loved one needs to hear, I do ask a lot of questions, such as,

What is your name?
How do you know the sitter?
How did you cross over?
What can I tell your loved one to let them know it's really you?

The souls don't need me to tell them how to make a session meaningful. They know what their loved one needs to hear, so their typical response to my questions is, "Be quiet and tell them what I'm telling you." They repeatedly make it clear that they could care less if what share with their loved ones makes any sense to me. What they do care about is that the messages make sense to the person hearing them.

■ ■ ■

"Do you know who Laura is?" I asked Jolyn, who was at one of my open group session nights.

Jolyn was visibly stunned. "Yes."

"Living?"

"Yes."

"I'm being told that she's a friend of yours."

"Yes."

"A good friend."

"Yes."

"In fact, you two are *best* friends."

"Yes."

"I don't know if she's open to this sort of thing but would you mind telling her that someone, I don't know who this is, but someone wants to talk to her?"

Jolyn nodded. The reason she was even there that night was that a couple of weeks before I told a friend of *hers* that someone was asking for her. The idea that I even spelled her name, J_O_L_Y_N correctly is what convinced her to come in the first place.

When she told her friend that "someone" from the hereafter was asking for her, Laura belly laughed. She was an avowed atheist. "A guy who claims he can talk to dead people? Right… whatever!" She came to a group session anyway thinking it would be "cheap" entertainment. Since she didn't have to give her name at the door I didn't know she was Jolyn's friend. But a soul on the Other Side knew who she was.

■ ■ ■

"I have a soul coming through for you, a male figure. Like a father figure. Your father passed?"

She looked at me skeptically and nodded her head.

"I should tell you, I don't think that this is your father I have coming through. Not that your father isn't okay. I just don't sense that this is him. He's really goofy. I hope that doesn't offend you when I say this, because he's showing me the NASA symbol. He was either an astronaut or a 'rocket scientist' so he was extremely smart when he was here. The reason I said he was 'goofy' is that he's telling me really *bad* jokes that he thinks are hysterical!"

"Oh, my God," Laura thought to herself, "could he really be hearing from my Uncle Bob?' She was stunned.

"He thanks you for being here. He's telling me that you don't believe in this sort of thing." I looked at her and smiled. "He asked for you because he says that you know someone who has attempted to kill herself since his passing. More than once, as a matter of fact."

Tears filled Laura's eyes and she nodded.

"Well, would you please tell whoever this is that he wants to talk to him or her?"

"I will," she said quietly, trying to rationalize in her mind what just happened.

A few weeks later, at another group session I was giving, I was talking to a woman beforehand. I normally don't do this, but I heard a voice in my head telling me to ask who told her about me. So, I did,
She stared at me for a moment. It was more like a glare. "A friend," was all she said.

Later that night, when it was her turn to receive messages, two souls came through for her. I said, "I have another male figure coming through for you. He tells me that he's your brother. Do you understand this? Just say yes or no, please."

She didn't say either. She simply nodded her head. Her face was pinched, determined not to give anything away with her facial expressions.

"Did your brother work for NASA? He's showing me the space agency's symbol. I hope this makes sense."

She nodded her head again.

"He's talking about someone who has tried to commit suicide since his passing. Not once, but a few times. Do you know who he's talking about?"

Tears came to her eyes, again.

"His wife. Your sister-in-law."

"Yes," she said.

"Are you still in touch with her?" I asked.

"Yes."

"Would you tell her that he wants to speak to her?"

"I will."

When the readings were over, she came up to me and introduced herself. "My name is Sue," she told me. "The 'friend' I told you about is my daughter, Laura."

I had *no idea* who she was talking about.

"THAT'S ME."

I received an email from a woman asking if she and her mother could have a reading with me. We set one up for three months away at my office.

When the day of her appointment finally arrived, she was with her mother, young son, and her fiancé. "You must all be willing to hear from whomever comes through," I told them. Since this wasn't a group session, I didn't want to have to do a reading for the mother, another one for the daughter, and still another one for the fiancé. They all agreed, so I began.

I gave them my usual rules -

- Don't tell me who you're hoping to hear from by either name, or relationship.
- The souls know what you need to hear, so no questions. Be open to listening to what's coming through.
- Keep your feedback to a minimum answering with simply a "yes" or a "no."
- Make the soul or souls coming through prove themselves to you, don't make what they say to you "fit." A "circle" will always be a circle, and a "square" will always be a square.
- What doesn't make sense to you now, may make sense to you later in the session, or even after the session is over.
- The names given could be someone either living or deceased.

"I have a male energy coming through for you," pointing at Dawn. "He's coming across as a father figure. Your father passed. Yes?"

"Yes."

"You live here in Colorado, but did your family live somewhere else at one time? He keeps pulling me back east... to the East Coast. Does that make sense?"

"Yes."

"Okay... good. But I'm confused here. He's showing me the NASA emblem, but at the same time he's showing me land, like a farm... still on the east coast."

"He worked for NASA, but when he retired he bought several acres of land that we lived on," Dawn confirmed.

"He was highly regarded in NASA. Very well-known there."

"Yes."

"I mean *very* well known. He received awards for his contributions to the space program."

"Yes."

"He admits he was a bit of an 'oddball.'"

Both she and her mother laughed at this. "Yes." They both nodded

And so it went... when suddenly I heard something that I hesitated to even share. "He's talking about someone trying to take their own life. Not once or twice, but several times. Once by a gunshot to the head. Do you know who he's talking about?"

"Me," her mother said. She had been sitting quietly during the session for the most part. "That would be me," she answered calmly.

I looked at her stunned. I wasn't sure she understood what I had just said, or that I understood what she just said. It took me a moment to ask, "I'm sorry?"

"I'm the one he's talking about. I've tried to kill myself... more than once. You're right."

As she was telling me this, I was even more surprised by how calmly she was confirming this piece of evidence. Then tears began to fill her eyes. "I miss him so much," she continued. "I just want to be with him. I want to see him again."

"You will," I said. "I *promise* you that you will. And when you do, it'll be as though the last time you saw him was just a moment ago. But he wants me to tell you that this is *not* the way to do it. You're still here for a reason."

"When will I see him again?" she asked.

"When you've learned the lessons that you came here to learn, and teach the lessons you came here to teach. Your husband wants me to tell you that until then, he's only a thought or a whisper away. He's closer to you now than he ever was when he was here.

He also wants me to tell you he loves you. I want you to notice that I didn't say he 'loved' you. He said he *loves* you."

After the session ended, I did something I don't normally do. I played a song from them by Eric Clapton, *Tears in Heaven*. I was inspired to bring the C.D. with me that morning, and now I understood why. It was a great message for Dawn's mom.

As I walked them to the office door I noticed it was past 7 p.m. and I knew that they had a two-hour drive back home. "Are you going to stop somewhere for dinner?" I asked.

"Yes, we're going to my Aunt Sue's home. She wants to know how this went."

"I don't know who she is," I said.

"Yes, you do. She came to you for a reading. Sue Rodefer."

I shrugged my shoulders. I typically don't remember what was said during a reading once it's over, let alone the sitter's name.

"You know... Laura's mom!"

Suddenly, everything came back to me, starting with a reading I did in which I asked the sitter if she had a friend named, Jolyn, several months before. I realized for the first time who was coming through for Dawn and her mother that night was - Charles, a.k.a., "Uncle Goofy." By the grace of the Eternal Light of Love, that same soul orchestrated a series of sessions to be able to tell his wife, that night, that they would be together again, but to wait until it was her time.

Several months later, I received an email from Dawn. It was the kind that people send to their families towards the end of the year talking about what happened during that year. She talked about her mom, and how she was feeling much better. She seemed happier than she had in a long time. Dawn wrote that she even heard her mother singing Christmas carols.

DIAMOND 'LIL, UNCLE GOOFY AND TOR-TILL-LAS

Let me start by saying that before I met with Anthony I was an atheist and more skeptical and cynical than anyone I knew. The only reason that I saw Anthony was one of my best friends saw him and he asked if she knew someone by the name of Laura. He said that someone wanted to talk to me. My friend was a skeptic as well before she met Anthony so when she told me to go I thought I would go for laughs. I had seen a medium for fun before and she was a joke. I had no expectations whatsoever and never dreamed that my life would be so changed after my visit.

Anthony started by saying that someone was coming through and identified himself as a space engineer. Anthony said he was "goofy." He said the man kept telling jokes that he would laugh at but weren't as funny to everyone around him as they were to him.

That floored me as my Uncle Charles would call me on the phone and when I answered he would say "Hi Laura, this is Uncle Goofy" and that was his style of joke telling. He would always tell jokes that he would laugh at but others wouldn't laugh as hard as he would. My Uncle also worked as an engineer for NASA.

Then a man came through that was wearing a coat which he was very proud of. He kept saying "I don't know why nobody else likes this coat." My father won a purple sports coat at a sales convention and I would always tease him about how ugly it was. He wore it with pride and couldn't believe that as I thought it was so hideous. It was a stand-out moment for me as I will never forget that sports coat and how much pride my Father had in it.

Anthony asked about my Aunt who had made several attempts at suicide. My Uncle Goofy's wife had made several recent suicide attempts, including a gun in which she shot herself from under her chin. Anthony asked about someone recently attempting suicide and made the hand gesture of a gun and put it under his chin as that is what he was seeing. My Uncle wanted to get a message to my Aunt as to not commit suicide as she hadn't learned her lessons yet.

During my next visit, Anthony said a man kept saying "Wizard." I told him that I had no idea what Wizard meant and to please move on. Anthony tried to move on but the word "wizard" kept coming up in the reading. I later spoke with my Mother and said that Anthony kept hearing the word wizard and she immediately knew it was my Uncle as he won the only Wizard award ever given by NASA.

In this same visit, Anthony said that someone kept saying the word tor-till-la which meant nothing to me. Confused, I told him to move on as I didn't have any association to the word tor-till-la. Later I spoke with my Mother about the word tor-till-la and how it kept coming through in my session. My Mother instantly told me that my father always pronounced the word tortilla incorrectly and it was a big joke between them. A couple of days before I saw Anthony my brother and my Mom were talking about my Dad. My Mom was laughing and said that my Dad never pronounced tortilla correctly. He would always sound out the LL's.

My Father said that before he died my Mom asked, "What will I do without you?" He replied, "You will be fine." That is exactly what was said one day as my Mom and Dad were sitting at the kitchen table. I never knew about this conversation and the wording was verbatim.

My Father said that I was a Tomboy and he always wanted me to be a girlie girl but he lost the battle which was so true. Once again, he would use those exact words....

When my Mother went to Anthony someone came through and was calling herself "Eddie". It took my Mom a while to remember that her Mom used to call her Cousin Elsie, "Eddie." She said that my Mom loved to play jacks and eat pancakes. Many years ago, Elsie was visiting her and my Mom was playing jacks and they had pancakes for breakfast.

The name "Diamond Lil" came up in my Mom's session as well. My Mom said it was from her Dad because when she was a teenager she would play poker with my Dad and her Dad nicknamed my Mom "Diamond Lil."

Anthony has changed my life. I now know that there is life after what we know as death. I now know that God exists and thank God daily for guiding me to Anthony.

Laura Rodefer

Anthony's note – The death of a loved one is devastating no matter what the circumstances are that led to their passing, but it's especially so when someone crosses themselves over. In our society, grief is still taboo. You're expected to get on with your life, and show a happy face soon after something has happened, whether is a relationship or marriage ending, losing a job or career, or a loved one.

You need to understand that a medium is not a therapist, and a reading, while it may be helpful, is not meant to replace therapy. People come to me wanting to know that their loved ones are okay, especially those who committing suicide. I can tell you that they are. But anyone can read a "new age" book and tell you. The real job of a legitimate medium is to provide evidence that they really are discerning your loved one by providing evidence that only you would know.

A session with me, or any medium, will not "fix" you, or heal your heartache. It can help you to know that death is not the end of life, love or relationships, but you still need to honor the journey of grief that you're on. At best, a reading will let you know that you're *not* alone when you do.

Having said that, with so many people claiming to be a "medium" these days, I'd like to suggest that if you do seek out a medium, the best way to find one is word of mouth.

Even so, I still encourage you to be skeptical during your session. Just as Laura was when she came to see me. That's what I love about her story, and why I wanted to share it with you.

THE TREADMILL

People who have been caught in the wake of a suicide have told me that they must use every ounce of their strength to fight against being swept away by the churning chaos that they suddenly find themselves in. As they try to understand and take in what happened, they pray for the return of what used to be their normal routine.

Even the souls refer to the journey through sorrow as "walking on broken glass." While you might be aware of the "5 Stages of Grief," when someone you love, or someone close to you, takes their own life, all the guidelines go out the door.

Grief is not a linear process in which you go from the depths of hell to the joys of heaven the same way you'd ride an elevator from the basement to the penthouse suite. It's even less so when you lose someone to suicide.

It's a journey no one can understand unless they go through it themselves. You cannot explain it to someone who hasn't gone through it first-hand. It's impossible to understand the challenges – the unanswered questions, the feeling of shame, blame, and helplessness that comes in the aftermath of a suicide.

I don't think that there's anything that can prepare us for the death of someone we love, or know, who takes their own life. Someone who loses a loved one to suicide is not going to grieve the same way that they would if someone they loved died as the result of a long-term illness, or injury.

I've heard survivors talk about is how they play out different scenarios in their head, trying to figure what happened and what they could have done or said that would have changed things. Even those who have assisted a loved one in crossing over, talk about their guilt and doubt as to whether they did the right thing.

"If only I…."

"If I had listened…."

"I should have known…."

"Why didn't I say something?"

"If only I had called."

What's going on is that you are trying to regain control over the uncontrollable. But like walking on a treadmill nothing around you changes.

You cannot change what's happened, and I've heard souls tell their loved ones that they couldn't have stopped what was going to happen once they made their decision.

What they do say is that asking these questions, feeling guilty, or blaming yourself or someone else, doesn't add anything of value to your life or your soul, and it won't help you heal. They say that we need to get off the treadmill of, "Should have…, Would have…, Could have…," and begin the journey of putting one foot in front of the other knowing that we'll all be together again, one day, in the hereafter. And to hold on until that day comes.

"I'M NOT WHO YOU THINK I AM."

Devann was born on December 2, 1966. As a baby and a toddler, she was angelic looking. She had beautiful strawberry blonde hair. But you couldn't let her looks fool you. She was a firecracker.

She was 22 months younger than her brother and just loved being with him. As she grew older she developed a passion for soccer. She played on a traveling team, an Olympic development team, and her high school soccer team. Even though, while playing soccer she tore the ACL on both her right and left knees, she never once thought of giving up playing, and fought through each one of her injuries to come back and play again. Everyone agreed that she had a natural talent for the game and was amazing to watch her play.

Devann was well liked and had some amazing friends. She was very smart and witty. She was voted funniest girl in her Freshman year of High School. She was a bit of a "tomboy" in that she not only played soccer, but loved fishing, hunting, wakeboarding and four-wheeling. She competed in pageants, as well, as she grew and blossomed into a beautiful young woman.

When she was 12 years old her baby sister was born and I can honestly say that she loved her more than anything else in her life. She loved being a big sister, and the bond between them was amazing to see.

Devann had plans to go to college and wanted to work in the medical field but she wasn't sure if she wanted to be a physician or nurse practitioner. Her dream was to work in emergency medicine.

A perfectionist, she always pushed her to her limits, giving everything she had to whatever she did. She was on the Idaho Olympic development team for soccer the summer before she was in the 8th grade. That's when she tore her ACL. Out for an entire year due to surgery and rehab, she felt lost. Her friends continued to play, while she watched, feeling left out.

While she was recovering, she missed playing soccer her entire 8th grade year. It was during this time that she suffered kidney failure. Her doctors and I were baffled as to how this could have happened. She was asked again, and again, if she had taken an overdose of her meds, but she denied it. Her specialist didn't believe her, but her pediatrician had no reason to believe she did, and I never would have guessed that she had.

She was very sensitive to what other people thought about her, and she didn't feel like she always fit in. I wish that she could have seen herself the way we, her family, and everyone else did, but she didn't.

She tried out for the high school varsity team the start of her Freshman year, but since she hadn't played at all during the 8th grade she didn't make the team. She was devastated. I do believe it was during this period that she started to feel as though she was no longer a part of the same group of friends she used to belong to.

She tried out and made the Junior Varsity soccer team, and was even named the team captain. She continued to play on the traveling soccer team, and the summer before her Sophomore year, she tore her left ACL. Having gone through it once before, she wasn't afraid about having the surgery, knowing what she could expect from it, and her recovery.

After her left ACL was repaired, I found a letter she wrote that I will never forget. She wrote that she was struggling, again, with her friendships and feelings that she didn't fit in. She also wrote that her kidney failure was self-induced. I was devastated, of course, and got her into counseling right away.

We went to her pediatrician and told him everything, as well. He started her on medication and things seemed to be getting better. She made new friends, started hanging around a different group of people and gave us the impression that she was happy.

She could not play soccer her Sophomore year due to her being in recovery from her surgery on her left knee. But she played in her Junior and Senior years.

During the summers after her 10th grade and 11th grade she went to a program called Upward Bound. It's a college credit based program and she seemed to be enjoying it. During her second summer, there she called me, in tears, saying that she missed home, and that she and her friend were fighting. I was surprised to hear this because she and her friends were super close. I thought that perhaps they were spending too much time together at the Upward Bound program. I asked her if she wanted me to come and get her and she said no, that she was feeling sad and her friend wasn't being very supportive. She wouldn't tell me any more than that.

When she came home from Upward Bound she began playing soccer right away. She and her friend weren't spending time together anymore. I would ask questions, but all Devann would say was that her friend wasn't there for her. I decided not to push it thinking that she would tell me what happened sooner, or later. I could tell though that this was hard for her, and I did my best to let know that I was there for her when she needed to talk.

She didn't seem depressed. She continued to receive good grades in school. She had friends spent time with, and she had a boyfriend, as well.

After soccer season ended her Senior year, she came to me and said that she was going through a difficult time again. She was almost 18 years and didn't want to see a pediatrician, so I booked an appointment with a nurse practitioner. I made an appointment with the counselor she had seen before, but she told me that she wanted to see a female counselor instead.

The weekend before she died she asked me if she could go to a party. I agreed to let her go even though I knew that this group of friends liked like drink. I didn't approve of this sort of thing but I had the kind of relationship with my children that if they ever did drink they needed to tell me and not keep it a secret. I wasn't worried about Devann though since she had a strict code for herself as a soccer player, and part of it was that she didn't drink. Even so, she did tell me she was planning on drinking that night.

Around 2 a.m. that night she came home with her friends, and was very upset. I could tell she had been drinking, but when I tried to ask her what was wrong she didn't want to talk about what happened. I let her visit with her friends and when they left I went back to her bedroom. She told me that she just wanted to go to sleep.

The next day she told me that she went to the home of the friend she spent the summer with at Upward Bound. When she got to her friend's house, she texted her. Her friend let her in her house, and then started to tell her what a horrible person she was. I asked Devann exactly what was said, but she wouldn't tell me.

She had a doctor's appointment the next day. She told me that she wanted to go to it by herself. I asked her if she wanted me to go and just sit in the lobby, and she said no. Since she was almost 18 years old, I understood she wanted her privacy, so I agreed to let her go by herself.

She called me after her appointment and said that the plan was to start Devann on birth control pills to regulate her hormones. Then in a couple of weeks, if she was doing okay, they would start her on anti-depressants, but they didn't want to do both at the same time. I'm a registered nurse, myself, and I told my daughter I thought it was a good plan.

The next morning Devann asked me if she could stay home from school. I told her that I didn't think it was a good idea since she had just missed a week of school having gone to Alaska to accept a scholarship. She looked tired and sad, but she agreed. She got up, put makeup on, and went to school.

That night, when I came home from work, she was watching television with her sister. The three of us talked, and Devann told me that her one of her friends came up to her car at school and told her that she wished she couldn't remember them ever being best friends, and to tell me that my daughter is a horrible person. I didn't understand why her friend would say that, and Devann wouldn't tell me what was going on between them. I told her to give it some time that by the time graduation got closer that hopefully they'd be able to talk.

When I woke up in the morning Devann wasn't in the bathroom getting ready the way she normally was. I looked outside and saw her car, so I went to her bedroom. Her door was locked. I knocked on the door, and called out her name. She didn't answer. I became afraid, and knew immediately that something was wrong. I got my husband and my son. We banged on the door, and when she still didn't answer, my husband took the door off its hinges. That's when we saw my beautiful baby.

I remember screaming. I remember her dad screaming. I remember her brother screaming.

She was wearing the necklace and bracelet her best friend had given her. All her friend's notes and pictures were underneath her.

She had written on her mirror, 'I'm not who you think I am. I'm not who you think I am. I'm not who you think I am. I'm not who you think I am.'

I knew she had been gone for a while. I ran down the hall and then I thought to myself, "I'm a nurse. I know how to save her. I turned around and ran back to her but I knew that it was no use. I just didn't want to believe it. I continued to scream. I felt as though I were dreaming. This just couldn't be real. This wasn't really happening. Not my daughter. Not my family.

Talking to her friends afterwards, and piecing everything together, I've concluded that Devann was struggling with depression. She didn't feel like she fit in. She was extremely hard on herself. Her friends said that she talked about waking up in the middle of the night crying. Crying over her friendships. Crying because she felt like a horrible person. She told a couple of her friends that she was suicidal. One of her friends was shocked and thought that people really didn't do that sort of thing.

Devann struggled with feelings of abandonment... that her friends would leave her and that she'd be alone. After her passing, I received countless note cards from her friends and classmates. They talked about how they loved her smile, and her laugh. I heard many stories about how well liked she was. She wanted to make sure everyone was having a good day, and if she saw someone was having a bad day, she would do her best to cheer them up. Unfortunately, her low self-esteem and depression took away her ability to see how loved she was.

Between the time of February 2013 and July, 2015, I lost five close family members. First, my grandfather, 5 ½ months later, my mother-in-law passed away. A year later my brother in law died, then my daughter. Seven months later, it was my mother's time to leave.

Of all of them, nothing compares to the grief of losing my child. And the way she left only compounds the pain we feel.

Since then, our journey has been tough, to say the least. I can't really tell you how we've even survived. I sobbed and sobbed until I just felt numb. The two weeks following Devann's death are hazy to me. I had to take anti-anxiety medications, and meds to go to sleep. Even then, I was only able to sleep a couple of hours a night at the most. I remember thinking and asking myself, "Is this a dream?"

I can say that I wouldn't have gotten through it if it weren't for the help of my family, friends, and my church. They took care of the funeral arrangements. My husband took care of the burial. He picked out a beautiful baby blue casket for Devann. She said at one point that when she died she wanted to be cremated, but I just couldn't do it. I couldn't stand the thought. I hope she understands why.

We stayed with my friend for over a month until we found a rental home to live in. I was verbal about my grief. I cried and needed to talk. I needed support. I was an emotional mess.

My son was angry, or I should say, I felt he was. He thought she could have come to any of us. In fact, one night she was upset and he asked if she was, and she told him no.

She even acted offended he would even ask. This really hurt him because they were only 22 months apart and had always been there for each other.

My 5-year-old daughter on the other hand is a clown. She tried to make everyone happy. She was hyper and silly. This was so hard. As parents, we were like zombies. We could barely talk without sobbing and she wanted to get up and dance around. It was exhausting.

My husband and I started counseling right away. We started the kids as well, but our sessions were separate from theirs.

In my family, there wasn't any fighting. We didn't say mean things to one another. The last thing we talked about was how picky of an eater she was, and how her little sister was too. We talked about some college choices. It was supposed to snow and her Dad told her to be careful when she drove to school in the morning. That was it.

I don't remember telling her I loved her before going to bed, and now I wish I did.

Amber Anderson Mauer

THE HEALING PLACE

In much the same way that newborn babies need to be touched and held to not only thrive, but even survive, we need to feel that we have a sense of purpose and that we're valued for who we are. If we're missing that, as I've said before, our souls begin to weaken, making it harder to face the challenges of everyday life.

One soul came to me during a reading dressed as a clown. After his wife told me that he wasn't one, either as a hobby or professionally while he was alive, I interpreted what I was seeing as him showing me was that the smile on his face, the success he achieved, with all its trappings, was masking the pain he was feeling inside. Despite "having it all," he still felt despondent, unhappy, unfulfilled, and alone. These feelings were symptoms of an *illness* he felt in his heart that he didn't recover from.

When I heard this, it reminded me of how Robin Williams left us, and how people called him "selfish." A friend of mine, who calls herself a "psychic coach," said that she couldn't understand how someone with all his success, all his money, and all the people who loved him could do such a thing.

Fortunately, the Eternal Light of Love, and the souls do understand. When a soul enters the hereafter after taking their own life, he or she is immediately taken to a place to rest, reflect, and heal from the pain that caused them to do what they did.

I've been told by the souls that our pets are the closest thing to the Eternal Light of Love on this physical plane we currently live in because they love us without any conditions, and forgive us without question. Which explains why, when souls who have taken their own life over are in this "resting station," their only companions are gentle animals, and often, they are their furry family members whom they knew and loved during their life here on the earth.

I was explaining this to my friend Donna whose ex-boyfriend, Rene, committed suicide more than 30 years before. "I already knew that," she told me. "After he killed himself he came to me in a dream. His head was bandaged (he killed himself by shooting himself in the head), and he had Christine, his cat, who had passed away after he did. He told me he wanted me to know that he was healing and feeling better about himself. He was standing in a beautiful green field, and he really did seem to be happier."

That didn't stun me. What did surprise me was that Donna dreamt this twenty-four years after Rene crossed himself over.

It's important to keep in mind that on the Other Side, souls are allowed all the time they need to heal. When you hear someone telling you that you won't see your loved one who transitioned this way after you pass, it's probably because they're still in that place where they are healing and by themselves, until they're ready to see the souls of those they love in the hereafter.

But they don't do it in some dark, gloomy place where they're unable to see the Eternal Light of Love, or feel its joy. Anyone claiming to be a "medium" who tells you otherwise is someone you need to run away from. Do not listen to them.

If you think about it, this makes as much sense as someone going to the hospital because they're sick and having the doctors and nurses punishing them for feeling that way; making them sit in some dark, dank, filthy room for being ill to begin with. Yet this is exactly what some religions and so-called mediums would have you think!

The opposite is true according to what I've heard the souls in the hereafter say. According to those who take their own lives, they are treated in a very specific, and special way. The suffering they endured while they were here being acknowledged, it's understood that what they did appeared to the only way out of their constant confusion and pain. The Beautiful One understands this. Which is why they're treated with dignity, respect, compassion and love - not contempt, and condemnation.

When the souls talk about death, they refer to it as simply being a threshold between this life and an even greater one we return home to. They talk about it being as easy as going through a doorway from one room to another. In fact, it happens so quickly and easily that I've heard many souls say they didn't even realize what had happened until they saw their loved ones who had gone before them, greeting them, and leading them to the Eternal Light of Love to begin a review of the life they lived and the lessons they learned, and missed.

I knew from experience that the souls, including those who took their own lives, could communicate immediately. Jasmine, the young woman who insisted that I write my first book, *Communication from the Other Suicide*, hung herself on Christmas day, just a few months before. I had always assumed that she had already gone through her healing process and life review, *before* she communicated with her loved ones using me to give her a human voice.

I was wrong. It wasn't until much later, while I was writing this book, that I understood what really happens when someone does this, crosses over to the hereafter.

It happened when I woke up one morning just as the dark of night was starting to give way to the light of a brand-new day. I was comfortable and warm laying underneath my comforter. When I opened my eyes, I saw Bentley was lying next to me, looking back at me with unconditional love.

I laid there thinking, and praying, about my life, the people in it, and the day ahead. As I was laying there I heard, "This is very much like what someone who commits suicide goes through when they arrive in the Other Side. The darkness of the hurt and pain which drove them to do what they did is comforted by the unconditional love of the Divine which envelops them like the blanket you're lying under now. The more that they heal, the brighter their surroundings become, just as the rising sun pierces the morning darkness. Their only company are animals who will remain with them until they are ready to be assisted by souls who are able to help them understand why they did what they did, and help them heal. Only when they are ready will they see the souls of their loved ones who are waiting for them, and go through their life review during which they will have to come to terms with what their early exit means for them in terms of their growth."

If a loved one of your loved ones has taken their own life, please know that they are at peace, and are watching over you from a special place in the hereafter. If *anyone,* or any book, tells you otherwise, neither they, or it, are not worth your time, or attention.

THEY NEED YOUR PRAYERS

The first time I remember a soul who took his own life was coming through to me was during my first paid group session, at a birthday party of all things. I was doing readings when a soul came barging in, energetically speaking. To say that this guy was a jerk is an understatement. I looked at one of the people at the party, a woman named Laura, and told her, "I have someone here named Dennis who's insisting he needs to talk to you."

She nodded, but said, "I don't want to hear from him."

I couldn't blame her. Like I said, this guy was an *asshole*, and I told her so. She nodded. I told her that I sensed that there was drug abuse involved. She nodded again. I heard a gunshot suggesting, to me, that he ended his own life.

Tears came to her eyes, and she softly said, "Dennis, I don't want to talk to you." I could see how upset she was so I ignored him, and moved on to do another reading. I'll never forget the anger I felt coming from him. "Talk about being a pair of brown shoes at a black-tie party," I thought to myself.

A few weeks later I was doing a reading in a private session for her. By that time, I'd forgotten the unwelcomed "visit" during the party. "Do you take the name Dennis, living or deceased?"

She nodded her head.

"Deceased."

"Yes."

"A boyfriend? Significant other to you when he was alive?"

"Yes."

"I have to tell you, he's coming across as not being the nicest guy when he was alive. He's telling me he's the same guy who came to you at the party wanting to talk to you, but you sent him away."

Nods again. "Please tell him I don't want to talk to him."

"He abused drugs?"

"Yes."

"And you."

"Yes. That's why I don't want to talk to him."

It wasn't until I psychically heard a gunshot, again, that I remembered who he was. "Look," I told him silently, "she doesn't want to talk to you. You need to leave." And he did.

After the session was over and she left my home, Dennis came back to me again. I hadn't learned the "art" of psychic self-defense yet, and couldn't believe how pushy he was.

"I'm sorry for coming across to you the way I did," he began. This time, his energy was sincerely apologetic, so I listened. "If I hadn't, she wouldn't have known it was really me."

I've since learned that when a soul comes nearer to us, it often assumes the same personality it had when it was here during a reading. I've also learned that *after* they complete their life review, there's a transformation that takes place as they understand that they begin to drop all the defensiveness they developed when they were here to simply survive, because it's no longer necessary in the hereafter.

"You heard her," I responded. "She doesn't want to hear from you. She might in the future, but not right now. She's just not ready."

"I know. I just wanted to tell her I'm sorry for the way I treated her and to ask her to light a candle for me. I'm so close to moving up to the next level here. I need her forgiveness to do it though."

"Okay, I'll tell her," I promised, "but I can't make her do anything she doesn't want to do."

Dennis seemed to understand. He thanked me and pulled his energy away.

I called Laura on her cell phone, but my call went to voice mail. When I'm doing a session, I insist that phones be turned off, or at least silenced if the sitter is using their phone to record their reading on it. I left a message relaying what Dennis wanted.

About an hour later, Dennis came back to me. He was beaming. "Thank you. And please tell Laura I said, 'Thank you, and I love you.'" He pulled his energy back again, and my phone rang. Laura was calling me. When I answered, I could hear she was sobbing.

She told me that she was driving home thinking about the reading and how Dennis barged in a second time. She had a sudden urge to pull off the highway using an offramp far from her home.

"I turned right and a couple of blocks later I saw a Catholic church and drove into the parking lot. I'm not a Catholic, and I've never been in that church, but I had this urge to go inside and light a candle for Dennis. I didn't know where the candles were, so I had to ask. I lit the candle, told Dennis I forgave him, and said a prayer for him.

It wasn't until I got back in my car that I saw that you left a message for me, and *that's* when I heard your message from Dennis!"

I told her that he had come back to me and relayed the messages he left with me. At that point, we were both in tears.

I'm sharing this story with you because it makes the point that those who do cross themselves over still need our prayers, and our forgiveness, which are like spiritual hugs for them, not our anger. When one person forgives, two people are freed. Pray for them so that they can heal, and so that you can, as well.

HIS INNER DEMONS WON

I'll never forget that day. I heard the phone ring. My brother Dan was calling. He wasn't someone who called a lot because he didn't care for talking on the phone. I knew something was wrong, I just didn't know what.

"Hi Dan, what's up?" He let out a huge sigh and struggled to speak. "Dan? What's wrong?"

"Mair," he sighed again, "I don't know how to tell you this, but dad died."

My world came crashing down around me. "Wha... what? How? When?" I was shocked, and couldn't stop shaking. Dan told me that the coroner said it appeared he'd passed four hours before.

When he didn't show up at the Christmas party in his apartment building, his friend Peggy went to see if he was okay. She knocked on his door, and found it strange that he didn't answer. So, she checked the parking lot to see if he was gone. No, his car was still there. She went back to his apartment and knocked again. Still, no answer.

She went back to the party to see if she had missed him somehow. People asked her where he was. She had no idea, and everyone began to become concerned. Peggy found the maintenance man, who decided to call the police. They entered dad's apartment, and found him on the couch. The police officer checked his vitals, and called for the coroner.

"Oh, my God, Dan," I said, barely able to breathe. "I just talked to him two days ago!"

"Mair," Dan said quietly. "Dad committed suicide."

Even though my father told me he felt he had reasons to take his own life, I was still in shock. I wanted to believe that he'd get over them, and wouldn't do it. But he did. Should I have tried to talk him more? Should I have taken him more seriously? Was there something I could have said? Should have said, that would have made him change his mind?

I admit I grieved his death differently than my mother's grandmother's, and aunts. These women were very sick physically, and suffered terribly. I had a great deal of difficulty letting go. I felt I needed more time with them.

My dad, on the other hand, talked openly about wanting to end his own life. I tried to talk him out of it, but he was fighting with inner monsters who were getting the better of him. The way he treated my mom and me when I was growing up was horrific. There were beatings, threats, and worse.

Another one of his demons was his health. He suffered a stroke that weakened him to the point of being helpless. It took away most of his ability to speak, and he had to learn how to walk again. It was two years before he could do things for himself again. Despite all of that, he was still the same as he was before his stroke, temper and all.

A year later my stepmother, and my brothers left him to take care of himself. After that, his disposition softened a lot. He became the dad I'd always wished I had when I was a child.

When I got the call that he was gone, the walls came crashing down around me. I cried for the dad I finally got to know as an adult. The one with the sparkling blue eyes, and easy laughter. The one who loved me, and cared about me for the last ten years.

Yes, I grieved, but I also had to come to grips with the fact that he chose to commit suicide. There's nothing anyone could have said or done to stop him. If was his way of winning the fight he had with the demons that were tormenting him. It was the only way he felt he could finally quiet them down.

I met Anthony Quinata one night at a seminar he was presenting here in Erie, Pennsylvania. He talked about the afterlife, and how we're never alone. We may not be able to see our loved ones but they are always with us. To prove what he was saying, he started doing readings and my father was one of those who came through.

When Anthony came to me and told me that my dad wanted to talk to me, all I can say is that his facial expressions, the tone of his voice, the things he said and the way he said them… it was almost as though I were hearing my father himself. I thought I was going to faint and had to hold on to my friend who came with me for support.

My father was asking me to forgive him for the things he had done to me and my mother. I thought to myself, "I can't. Not now."

Long after the seminar, I kept thinking what Anthony told me. That part of my father's journey on the Other Side was to help me along in my journey here. He was asking for forgiveness so that I would be at peace, not just with him, but with myself.

It took several months but I finally did find it in my heart to forgive my father. Anthony was right. The burden that I'd been carrying around for years was gone when I finally did let it go. Now, I talk to, and pray for, my father every day.

Daddy, I love you. I miss you. I wish you were still here.

Marianne Shotto

MOURNING HAS BROKEN

Rick told his wife, Sandy, during her reading with me that once he decided to take his own life, he experienced a peace his hadn't felt in a long time. In his mind, he knew that he had made the right decision, and that choice was death. After that he went out to wash his truck, thinking about the good times he had in it, driving it off road with his son to some remote spot where they could go fishing, or scaring his friends with the way he drove. The more he reminisced, the more content he became. He found himself happier than he had been in a long time.

Not wanting to lose that feeling, after he finished washing his car, he walked back into his house, and past his wife, without saying a word. He then went upstairs and shot himself in the head.

"He did love that truck," she confirmed for me. "I can still remember looking at him out the window while he was washing it that day. He looked so happy. So, peaceful. I thought that whatever was bothering him was over. I had my husband back."

Ten years later, she still lives in the same house, and his truck still sits in the driveway, where he left it, untouched.

After a long pause, she looked at me and said, "I keep the truck because that's the way I want to remember him. Not the way I found him afterwards. I've been told by people that I need to sell it and move on with my life, but they just don't understand. This is the way I'm moving on *through* my life."

I'm not sure anyone is ever really prepared for a loved one to take their own life. When it happens, the grief, the whirlwind of primitive emotions, causes us to lose all our bearings, having no clue as to where to go or what to do. It's like being caught up in a tornado with little or no warning, and no time to prepare.

You can become lost in the feeling that grief is something that happens to you. Or you can do what the souls suggest you do, and that is to consciously choose to see it as, "mourning is something I'm doing to heal."

When life feels out of control, and it's going to while you're on this journey, whether it happened yesterday, or 30 years ago, you *do* have control over *how* you'll mourn. Just knowing that can be very empowering. As I mentioned before, I'm not a therapist, a psychologist, or a grief counselor. But I want to share with you some of the things I've learned speaking with those who lost a loved one to suicide, and the souls themselves.

It's a journey.

While there are some commonalities in the process, we don't all mourn the same way. The false belief that death is death, whether it comes suddenly, as the result of a long-term illness, or someone we love takes their own life, and that we grieve them the same way is just that, a myth. Recognize it as such, and don't give in to the demands of others that you should deal with your feelings and emotions in the same way as someone who loses a loved one to a disease, or injury.

It's not important that your journey through sorrow is the same, or different, from someone else's. What is essential is that, like Sandy in the story above, you recognize your own unique pathway through the pain you're feeling, and honor that.

Feeling crazy is normal.

In our modern culture, when someone becomes overwhelmed by their feelings, we medicate them to protect them and help them function "normally." We're so afraid of feelings, drugs are often prescribed, especially for women, to help people "cope;" to get them through a hard time, and past a difficult period. All that they're really doing is delaying the normal progression of grief. When we acknowledge, and let out painful emotions, we are participating in the process of healing. Going crazy (within reason) is normal.

There is no time limit when it comes to grief.

Jews are waiting for the coming of the Messiah sometime in the future. Christians believe that the Messiah came more than 2,000 years ago. Einstein proved that time doesn't exist... period.

It doesn't exist when it comes to grief either. There is no such thing as "grieving too long." Society and various religions may tell you the "rules" for grieving – how long you should grieve, what you should wear, how to behave, when we should talk about how our loved one died, and with whom. As with any death, but especially if your loved one took their own life, according to the souls you must find *your own way* through the journey back to embracing life again, but they'll be there with you every step of the way.

It's okay to be angry.

When I studied *Spiritual Direction*, I was taught that anger is an emotion that says, "I lost it, and I want it back." You lost a loved one. You probably didn't even see it coming. Chances are you didn't even get a chance to say good-bye.

Is it any wonder you're angry?

As an emotion, anger has a bad rap. It's an uncomfortable feeling for most of us, but it's one of the most important ones we need to express. Some people become angry with God, and as a "Spiritual Director," I tell people, "It's okay. Go ahead and scream at God. He/she can take it."

In Jewish Scriptures, there are several Psalms expressing anger at God about injustices. There's an entire book entitled, "Lamentations." So why are people, who are grieving the loss of someone they loved encouraged to "suck it up?" The Eternal Light of Love is not only divine mercy, but understands what you're feeling, and why.

If, however, you find yourself expressing anger in a way that's unhealthy, or out of control (i.e., destroying valuables, threatening people, hurting yourself or fantasizing about killing yourself, or someone else), then seek help from a professional therapist *immediately*.

Trust that you'll know when it's time to let go, and move on.

Your family and friends may be telling you that holding on to something that reminds you of your loved one will keep you stuck, but it's not true. Even someone's suicide doesn't erase the person or the impact he, or she, had on your life. It's okay to love them from a special place in your heart.

Treasure the memories of the love you both shared, the lessons you learned, and the gifts given and received. Remember the past, honor the present, and move into the future.

The only way out is through.

You cannot move through your grief unless you experience your sadness. Hiding it, or denying it, only prolongs it. It doesn't make it better.

Trying to avoid the pain you're feeling by keeping busy, cleaning the house, dusting furniture, scrubbing toilets and showers, organizing your closets, may alter the way you feel, but it's only temporary. The same applies to drinking alcohol, medications, or overeating, or whatever else you do to distract yourself from how you're feeling.

You can't journey through to the other side of your sorrow if you're in a blissful stupor. You can only do it with all your senses intact, and working, so you can face what happened head on. Numbing yourself only causes your grief to go underground, but sooner or later, it needs to find expression. As Carl Jung, the father of Depth Psychology said, "Bidden or unbidden, the gods will come."

The suffering you're experiencing is only useful *if* you learn something from it. Otherwise, according to the souls, the lesson is wasted, and the experience will not benefit you in any way either here, or in the hereafter.

Finding, and talking to someone who has also lost a loved one through suicide might help you. Someone who will lovingly listen if you need to talk is one way to hasten your healing.

You don't have to accept what happened.
Elisabeth Kübler-Ross (July 8, 1926 – August 24, 2004) was a Swiss-American psychiatrist, a pioneer in the study of near death experiences, and the author of the groundbreaking book *On Death and Dying* (1969), where she first discussed her theory of the five stages of grief.

The stages are:

- Shock
- Denial
- Depression
- Anger
- Acceptance

The "stages" she wrote about were meant for use by someone who is still living, but in the process of dying. They only partially apply to anyone who experiences the sudden death of someone they love. Especially when it comes to the idea of "acceptance."

When someone who is still alive is dying, *slowly*, they can learn to accept the reality of their approaching death, *slowly*. When we lose someone suddenly, as is the case with suicide, accepting their death is extremely difficult. The word "acceptance" seems to imply "approval."

Instead of trying to accept that your loved one took their own life, you're probably better off coming to a place in which you "acknowledge" what they did. Not only to yourself, but to others as well, which isn't easy considering the stigma that suicide has attached to it.

One woman I talked to told me that it's just easier for her to tell people who ask how her husband died that he suffered a massive heart attack. She often felt judged when she told people that he took an overdose of drugs as though they thought she was somehow to blame for what he did.

"Let them think what they want," I told her. "What they believe is not important. What *is* important is that you understand that the journey to healing, and learning the lesson you're being asked to learn, is through the pain of acknowledging what happened."

Forgive them. Forgive yourself.

Forgiveness happens when we quit wishing the past were different.

I'm not suggesting this because if you don't forgive your loved one, you're somehow keeping your loved one stuck in a holding pattern in the hereafter until you do. You're not doing it for them. You're doing it for yourself. Any guilt and shame you may feel over what happened is a form of self-judgment. Forgiving your loved one, and yourself, allows you to get off the treadmill of, "If only…."

When you forgive them for the pain they caused, you not only free yourself from the past, you're opening yourself up to being healed, and being happy again. You're also giving yourself permission to live in the present, and to grow in the future.

IT WAS ALL I COULD DO JUST TO BREATHE

I have a brother. His name is Adam John Walker. Adam was the kind of guy that would give you the shirt off his back. He had a strong moral compass and was a man with integrity.

Unfortunately, he was also the kind of person that always saw the "glass as half empty." This made life difficult for him because all he really wanted was to be loved and to love someone.

Adam believed he was alone in this world. For over a decade Adam self-medicated with addictions. It took a toll on his mind, body and soul.

January 16, 2012 was the worst day of my life. Nothing would ever be the same. Adam died by suicide. The world as I knew it had stopped. He expressed suicidal thoughts for over 15 years before that fatal day. He fought a long war. He was strong, but at 35, the drugs convinced him it was his only way out of the pain. A sister's love was not enough.

Losing someone to suicide makes grieving complicated. How does one begin to process this? It's not the same as if your loved one died in a car accident, or from cancer. I remember very clearly the confusion I felt. It was all I could do just to breathe. The rest of the world around me just kept on going...the sun rose every morning and the birds still chirped, but for me, it was like being frozen in time.

I didn't feel my brother or think he was trying to communicate with me until a month before the 3-year mark was approaching. He led me to Anthony Quinata, 1300 miles away. December 20, 2014 my life had changed yet again. The messages I received gave me the peace I so desperately needed. One of the many messages I got in my session with Anthony was that he knows now how much he was loved, and how much we tried to help him, even though he couldn't see, or feel it, when he was alive. He also let me know that he was okay.

And so, my spiritual journey towards my own peace began. There aren't many choices when it comes to Surviving Suicide. I chose "Acceptance."

Because of Adam's death, I have learned so many things. He taught me Unconditional Love never dies; that it is the most powerful emotion we have because it lasts forever. My session with Anthony confirmed for me that my brother is with me still, every day, watching out for me. I learned that the way I can honor my brother is to continue my life's journey. Adam let me know that he is on it with me, and will never leave me.

I also learned that every single day I wake up to see the sun rising every morning, and hear the birds chirping - that these are gifts from Heaven.

I will never be the same person I was before my brother's suicide, and I've come to accept that. I wish my brother could have found the peace on earth he so desperately wanted, and deserved, while he was still here. I do know, now, that he is moving towards finding it where he is.

For those of us he left behind, the grief we feel is a very dark, lonely place. I do the best I can to live with this sorrow. Every day I wake up now, knowing he is still with me, that he's okay where he is, and that I will see him again, does help.

Do I wish I never had to go through any of this? Yes...he is my brother and I love him deeply... in life and in his death; and until the time that we're together again in Heaven, I will hold him safely in my heart.

Summer Walker

THE LIE

The word suicide may be used on someone's death certificate, but it doesn't begin to address the nightmares that were going on in their mind.

Can depression, anxiety, PTSD, or mental illness kill someone?

You'd better believe it. They are illnesses that can be overwhelming for people. That's why I've never heard a soul express regret over what they did, any more than I've heard one say that they regretted passing from any other disease.

One of the things I've heard during readings I've done in which those who crossed themselves over have come through is that, *when we don't feel good about ourselves, our soul withers*. When we start to become despondent, it feels as though we have no purpose, or value – to others, or to ourselves. It feels like standing in a vacuum in the middle of space and everything is being pulled away. The universe becomes a very vast place, and the feeling of being very... very... very... *alone* is overwhelming.

They talk of feeling as though they're locked up behind a dark prison, isolating them, blocking out the light, making them unable to feel the love of family, and friends. Any sense of comfort and confidence they had is lost to them. The loneliness and terror of feeling worthless, unlovable, a burden to others, made them think that they were undeserving of even breathing.

What the souls who have done this want you to know is that if you're feeling this way, it's a lie. You have value. You are loved. You do matter.

Do not believe the story that you are worthless and unlovable. It lives, breathes, and can only exist when you isolate yourself from those who love you.

Talk about how you're feeling. Reach out, listen to, and trust the voices of those who love you. If you don't feel as though you can do that, reach out to someone you feel you can. Know that no matter what the lie tells you, if you bring it out into the open, you'll see it for what it really is.

The souls want you to know the truth: **you** are important.

There's a huge difference between thinking, "I'm depressed but I know that I'll get through this," and, "I'm depressed and this pain will never end."

The question to ask yourself isn't, "How can I end or numb this pain right now?"

Ask yourself, instead, "What is the meaning of this pain? What does it reveal to me? What am I being asked to learn from this? To understand?"

Pray, and ask the Beautiful One to reveal to you the truth of you who really are – no matter how magnificent it is.

Reach out. Pursue help. If you need it, get counseling, and/or medical treatment.

They want you to know that suicide doesn't end the pain. It only passes it on to others.

They want you to know that suicide is a mistake.

"LIFE DOES KIND OF MAKE SENSE."

It's not unusual for me wake up from a sound sleep, even at just before 4 a.m. Typically, it means that I'm being asked by the Eternal Light of Love to pray for someone. Or it could be a soul preparing me for someone who needed my help. In this case, it was both.

A few minutes later I heard my phone ding. Someone was messaging me on Facebook. "I'm not going to read it," I thought to myself.

"You have to," I heard a young female voice say softly.

I opened the message, and read it. It was from a woman named, Debbie. "I need to know what the souls think," she wrote.

"I'm not going to answer it," I thought.

"Please! You need to answer it!"

"What I need to do is get some sleep."

"Please talk to her! It's my mom, and she's thinking of doing something she shouldn't. She thinks it's what I want but it's not."

I sighed, picked up my phone, and wrote back to Debbie, "What do you mean?"

"My daughter Amy died a year ago; I miss her so much. I just want to kill myself, and I want her to tell me it's okay," she wrote back.

■ ■ ■

"I am a grieving mother here to share my story in hopes of giving someone hope.

On June 25, 2013, I found my daughter in the bathroom unresponsive, I performed CPR as best I knew how until the paramedics came which seemed to take forever. They tried everything they could and called time of death at 12:34 pm, that's when my life changed forever.

Amy was born on May 27, 1986. She was a very healthy baby full of energy. She loved life and matured quickly. By the age of 16 she had 2 cars and cherished them both. She worked long hours to pay for them. I showed her the finer things in life and how to appreciate the hard work you had to put into life to get things in return. Amy had some issues in the schools so I chose to homeschool her and she graduated at an early age and started college. Everything was great until July of 2008 when she was held at gunpoint and locked in a freezer to die at her work.

Luckily, she escaped that but then the struggles began. Her work placed her on Workman's Comp with meds and counseling. Three months later they stopped everything and Amy turned to opiates, then heroin. It was a spiral downhill from then on. Her friends stole all my jewelry and pawned it for money. Every day I received a phone call either from jail, a hospital or the police. Amy was constantly in trouble. I fought every day for her life putting her in detox clinics and rehabs. Nothing seemed to work.

In February of 2013 she woke up screaming nonstop, I tried to help and she barricaded herself in her room, threatening to slice her neck, I had no choice but to call the police. They called the SWAT team in. Amy was taken to the hospital to be sedated for only 3 days then released to the mental health hospital where they released her without my knowledge since she was over 21.

This sort of behavior continued until April 1 where she ended up on the wrong part of town and was brutally raped by 12 men. I found and rescued her and took her to the rape crisis center. Again, things spiraled downward. That evening she had another manic episode. I called 911 and the hospital told me once again there were no drugs in her system and hasn't been the last 6 episodes. That's when they told me she was schizophrenic.

I went home and wrote out everything that had happened in the last 5 years and came up with the fact that what triggered her schizophrenia was when she was locked in the freezer. She was again taken to the mental health hospital where I pleaded with them to keep her until they found a medicine that would control her condition. I stayed in my car outside the facility to make sure they didn't just let her go.

Amy came home a week later and was herself again. She was very happy, wanted to finish college and get on with life. We celebrated her 27th birthday and it was wonderful. I was so happy to have my daughter back. She explained to me that she heard voices in her head that told her to kill me but deep inside she knew that was wrong and that's why she barricaded herself in her bedroom so she couldn't get to me. I cried so hard and hugged her and told her we can get through this together.

Things were going great... finally. I had lost my job through this period and was then working two part-time jobs. There were many days I had to work double shifts, and then go back the next morning.

On June 25, 2013, I had only gotten two hours sleep between work, but continued to drag myself in the shower to get going to the next job. As I was driving to work something kept telling to turn around but I didn't listen, I kept driving. When I got to work, the feeling was so strong I decided to listen and asked to go home.

I called Amy to tell her I was on my way back home but she didn't answer, I figured she was still sleeping. I walked through the door and saw her bedroom light on, I looked in her room and she wasn't there, so I turned and looked in the bathroom and there she was slumped over the bathroom counter. I ran and picked her up. She was warm but lifeless. I had no idea what had happened until I heard something hit the floor. It was a syringe... a full syringe. I was confused. I called 911 and started CPR without luck.

When the paramedics couldn't revive her either I started screaming at the top of my lungs wishing it was me and not her. I was in denial for almost a year. I screamed at God; I became a recluse, and wished I would just die.

The pain was unbearable. I just lost my only child, my daughter, my best friend, all my future hopes and dreams. I would never see Amy get married. I would never be a grandma.

I laid in bed for two weeks screaming and crying. I never knew I had that many tears in me. I didn't eat or sleep. I was so confused and hated life.

I had to get back to work. I felt like I weighed a thousand pounds. It took everything I had to get out of bed and get in the shower. I just wanted to die.

I went back to work but hated everything. So many thoughts racing in my head. The vision of finding Amy haunted me every minute. I couldn't focus, I couldn't do anything. There were so many why's and what if's.

I wrote a list of ways to kill myself, but as I went over it I started crossing things off because going head on into traffic could have hurt innocent people. Blowing my head off with a gun would have left a mess for innocent people to clean up or worse yet I could have missed and became a paraplegic. Jumping off the highest building here could have left horrible visions in people's minds. I had to come up with something that didn't affect people.

I tried so many things to ease my pain but nothing worked. I talked to Amy constantly, then I started talking with mediums. That's how I met and started talking to Anthony.

They eased my mind that Amy was ok and all her suffering was gone. She told me it was just her time, nothing I could have done different would have changed her time of death. I thought so much about everything... things started to become clear.

I started reading books about the afterlife. The books helped a lot but nothing was going to bring Amy back... nothing. So, I still wanted to die. I prayed every day to die. Then I read more books about the afterlife which are written by people who claim to be able to talk to the souls. They seemed to be helping more.

I read a book about our soul's plan. I don't know if what I read is true, but nothing else made sense. After losing a child, all you have is faith because everything else is gone. So, I had to hang on to anything that would keep me moving forward.

I read in one of the books that if you commit suicide that your mind will stay in a bad state and I may never see Amy again. I read and reread that book over and over and realized I couldn't take that chance. As time went on I learned to cherish the time I did have with Amy and not to dwell on her death. It's a lot of work but I had no options.

Things were getting better a tiny bit every day. I had planned my suicide on the same day Amy died... one year later. I had my letter all written in a sealed envelope. I believe Amy, spirit guides, the universe, and whatever else came forward changed my thoughts in my head. I tore up the letter and kept moving forward.

I moved out from where me and Amy had lived together for 13 years. It was hard, very hard, but I did it. After I moved the cloud in my head started lifting. Things were starting to feel alive again. Now it's 2015 and life seems good again, but then here it comes... my dad was rushed to the hospital thinking it was a heart attack turned out to be stage 4 stomach cancer. My dad cried. He said, "I'm gonna die."

I looked in his eyes and said, "If I could trade places with you I would, believe me." He chose to go through chemo and radiation, but 3 weeks later he died. I was devastated at losing someone I loved once again. So here comes the grief wave again.

Now I am left to take care of my ill mother. She gained some strength from his death and seemed to come alive a bit. We went shopping together, went and got haircuts, manicures and pedicures. We went out to eat; we just had some good quality time. Then one day she told me she had a dream of my dad pulling her arm saying, "Come on, it's time to go."

Stupid me, not seeing things how they were. I just thought she was lucky to dream of him. I was in so much grief from my daughter and my dad dying that I didn't see reality. It's been 4 months since my dad passed and my mother's health is failing fast. I have her in and out of hospitals but they don't find anything. I placed her in a home care, a beautiful place, with lots of water fountains.

I couldn't help my mom 24/7, I am not a nurse but I was there as much as I could be. Each day her health was failing. Almost 2 weeks later I noticed my mom couldn't see me anymore... she didn't know who I was. She was talking to other family members who had already passed. She was calling out, "Mommy... mommy... mommy!"

I went home and researched the natural dying process. I saw what my mother was going through in black and white. Then I got the phone call the following morning that my mom had passed.

Oh, my God, here I am in grief again. I lost my family. I am alone in this cruel world. I just wanted to die!

So now I'm asking God, the high power, whoever will listen..., "What the hell is going on? I just buried my family and I'm alone. Just take me!"

I felt I had no purpose, why was I still here? Nobody should have to live with this much pain. I felt so lost.

Today, I'm still doing a lot of soul searching, and talking to my family that has crossed over. Except now I'm taking a different approach. I am determined to find the answer to a question my daughter asked me once and I find myself asking it all the time. "What's it all for?"

I want to know why. I saw my daughter, dad and mom die, all in different ways. The good that came from it was that I got to spend some quality time with each before the end came. I have those memories to live on with.

I am determined to know why the world is the way it is. I need to know the purpose of so many people suffering. I have learned a lot since being swallowed in grief, but I want to know more. I realize we don't have much control over things, but ourselves, so might as well take advantage of it.

My daughter kept fighting to the end, my dad kept fighting to the end and my mom kept fighting until the end, so I must keep fighting to the end. I have learned that our *time comes when it is supposed to. Each day we live in pain we must reach deep inside and keep fighting.*

We are to be loving, caring and compassionate. Pain is part of everyone's lives. We can't avoid it, and we can't suppress it. We must accept it, face it learn from it, and hopefully create something good from it.

I have changed. I seem to live more searching for answers from the Other Side. I see people who are materialistic, egotistical, and many other things, I should keep to myself, but you know what…, none of that matters. What matters is **LOVE***. Love is the only thing that never dies or goes away.*

Life kind of makes sense as I look back and see how the story has played out. It just leaves me with so many unanswered questions.

We all have a role as the story goes. May peace be with you all and I wish you much love and light.

Debbie Harris

WHY ME?

There was a king who had to leave his kingdom to conduct business in a far-off land. Even though he had advisors he trusted to help him with the day to day affairs of his kingdom, he decided that he would have his best friend rule in his place while he was gone, instead. Rather than being pleased, his friend was upset.

"Why are you so troubled?" his wife asked him. "This responsibility is a great honor! You should be proud that your friend trusts you to do this."

"I didn't ask for this!" her husband groaned. "His advisors who help him govern, and when they find out, they will become jealous, and grow to hate me. After that, who knows what will happen? Why didn't he give this responsibility to them?"

"Then tell him that you don't want the duty he's given you," his wife advised.

"I can't," her husband replied. "He is my friend, but he's still my king. Why did he choose me for this, though? Why me?" He went off to be by himself, and he wept.

When the king left, his friend's greatest fear came true. The king's advisors quickly grew jealous of him, and angry about not being given the responsibility of overseeing the kingdom in his absence. Day after day they asked him why he was chosen. Then, one day they surrounded him and began to beat him, leaving him broken and bloody, lying on the ground. The king, found him where he lay, having come home unannounced.

"What happened to you?" he cried out.

The man explained how the king's advisors beat him, angry that he was chosen over them to govern during the time he was gone.

"How many times did they hit you?" the king demanded to know.

"38 times, your highness," his friend sobbed.

The king turned to one of his assistants and told him, "Count out 38 pieces of gold, one for each time he was struck, and give it to him." He then walked away angry at what had happened to deal with those who hurt his friend.

As the king's aide counted out the coins the man cried, "Why? Why? Why didn't they hit me more?"

■ ■ ■

When it comes to the question of suffering, the souls have admitted to me that they don't have a good answer, except that it happens for our spiritual growth. We come here knowing that it's part and parcel of life here on earth. In fact, it's the very reason we choose to come here to begin with.

One day, I passed that same advice on to someone I was doing a reading for. They say that the reasons vary from person to person, but they all agree that there's a reason for everything that happens to us. *Everything* that happens.

Being Roman Catholic I was taught to offer up any suffering I experienced for the souls in "purgatory." I even offered that same advice to sitters who were talking about the suffering they were going through, as well. Then one day it hit me, we *are* in purgatory. This life is designed to allow us to grow spiritually by confronting us with our deepest fears, and offering us opportunities to let those anxieties go in a way that benefits both us, and all those around us.

Another thing they all agree on is that a reward awaits us for all the suffering we go through. One young woman who passed away due to a disease that caused her so much suffering that she said she wouldn't wish on her worst enemy. She told her parents during their reading that she would willingly go through it again for a small part of the joy which awaited her for enduring what she did.

I've always found it interesting that if a soul who has lived through physical, mental or emotional pain here, even mentions it, it's usually to assure their loved ones here that whatever the suffering they went through here, it ended the moment that they crossed over; but they talk about it as though it were a distant memory. When it is brought up, the soul's reaction is something along the lines of, "Oh yeah… that…"

THE REWARD

The souls frequently say that there are some things that they can't explain because we must experience them for ourselves. I've struggled with the idea of what the souls mean when they talk about being "rewarded" for all the struggles and suffering they endured, that we must all go through, while we are here on earth. Trying to explain to others what I, myself, didn't really understand made it even more frustrating. But I need to give credit to the Eternal Light of Love and the souls for being patient with me and waiting until they felt they could explain it to me in a way that I'll understand. In a way that I hope you'll understand as well.

It happened one morning while I was taking my dog Bentley for a walk thinking about this idea of being "rewarded," and wondering if there was a better word I could use, even though it was the word the souls use talking to their loved ones during sessions. That's when they reminded me of a story I read when I was in my 20's.

Sir Edmund Hillary was being honored in a banquet for his attempts to be the first man to climb Mount Everest, even though up to that time, all his efforts resulted in failure. On the wall behind the podium was a huge picture of the mountain. Hillary stood in the back of the room listening to the accolades being said about him, tears streaming down his face.

Everyone who saw this assumed it was because he was moved by what he was hearing said about him.

Suddenly, he ran down the aisle, up on to the stage, and stood in front of the picture beating it with the sides of his fist. "Everest, you beat me the first time, but I'll beat you the next time because you've grown all you are going to grow... but I'm still growing!"

With that he walked off the stage leaving a stunned audience behind. He later became the first man to climb Mount Everest.

I hadn't thought of that story for more than 30 years. Suddenly, the whole idea of being "rewarded" for what we go through in this life started to make sense.

When Hillary climbed to the top of Everest, it was said he "conquered" the mountain. I believe that in his mind, he was determined to conquer himself. He did it to grow from the experience, as you can see from this quote -

> *It is not the mountain we conquer but ourselves.*

Years later, I had a friend named Karen who decided that she wanted to run a marathon. Since she hadn't run in one before, she knew she had a lot of preparing to do. She bought books about running marathons, and then one morning she put on her running shoes and ran a block.

The next morning, she ran two blocks. The morning after that, three.

A friend of hers joined her thinking that she'd like to run in the same marathon that Karen was running in, but her heart wasn't really in it, so she stopped. But this was something Karen's *wanted* to do. She followed a strict training regimen, and a diet that was supposed to help prepare her for the run nutritionally.

She researched and bought the best shoes she could find. Every morning, she'd get up early and run. And she kept this up until she was running 10 miles a day, six days a week.

Nothing she did, she told me later, prepared her for the experience of running 24.2188 miles non-stop. At one point, she wasn't sure where she was distance wise so she called out to a man who was watching the runners, "How much farther?"

"You still have a long way to go!" he yelled.

"No! Don't tell me that!" she cried.

He shouted back, "Not far! Keep going! You're not far from the finish line!"

Then it happened. She bonked. She hit what marathon runners call *the wall*.

"Hitting the wall" is when sudden fatigue and loss of energy sets in, caused by the depletion of glycogen stores in the liver and muscles. It's a much-feared and discussed phenomenon in marathoning. It happens about 20 miles into a marathon. When it happened to Karen she told me that her feet felt as though they'd been turned into scuba fins. She became pre-occupied with the idea of just giving up and laying down on the pavement. She said that it was as though her body, her brain, and even her soul, had collapsed within her.

Runners say that when this happens that the race is *half* over.

"I didn't start this not to finish," she thought to herself and continued to put one foot in front of the other, looking down, knowing that sooner or later she'd cross the finish line. When she finally did, her friend Carla, who was supposed to be there to meet her at the finish line, wasn't there. Carla needed to find a bathroom and couldn't wait any longer.

I asked Karen how she felt when she finally reached the finish line and didn't see her friend standing there, cheering her accomplishment.

"I was disappointed," she said, "but I told myself that I didn't do it for her, or anyone else, for that matter. I ran the marathon for me."

I asked her if she thought she'd ever run another marathon. She shrugged her shoulders. "I did it for myself. I did it to see if I could. I'll probably do something different."

After the souls reminded me of these stories, I remembered a quote by Albert Camus - *In the midst of winter, I found there was, within me, an invincible summer. And that makes me happy. For it says that no matter how hard the world pushes against me, within me, there's something stronger – something better, pushing right back.*

We may never climb a mountain, or run in a marathon, but in a very real sense, we all face mountains and races in our lives. *Reaching the top of the mountain, finishing the race*, and discovering what we're made of is only the first of the rewards the souls talk about. Earning the right to greater levels of peace, joy and happiness on the Other Side for having gone through them is another.

And it only gets better from there.

ASK ANTHONY

He's Drudging Around the Other Side?

I work with a friend who communicates with departed souls. Her best friend's deceased grandfather came through while she was driving and told her that his granddaughter (my co-worker's friend) was pregnant and it came to pass as being true.

The son of another coworker took his own life and came through to her and she described him as drudging around in perpetual sadness. This does not sound like it resonates with what you mentioned regarding the topic of suicide.

Also, do souls come through to help and guide you when answering email questions, or are your answers based on what you can recall from past experiences?

Mike

Thanks for writing to me, Mike.

I call myself a *psychic medium* because it was the first term I'd ever heard, or read, used about the ability I discovered I had. But there is a huge difference between a psychic and a medium.

Depending on how they perceive information, a psychic can sense information from the vibrational energy of the person they're "reading," including things like life direction, upcoming births, and how someone close to them passed away.

As a medium, I don't read the sitter's energy but *discern* the messages I hear, see, feel, and even smell from souls who have crossed over to the Other Side. I cannot pass along anything I don't hear from a soul during a session.

In all the years that I've been doing this (long before it was in vogue for someone to call themselves a "medium") I've never heard a soul who crossed themselves over say that they were "drudging around the hereafter in perpetual sadness." I have heard souls talk about the healing they were doing, but they talk about doing it in a place of peace, love and serenity.

Several years ago, I did a session for a woman and her daughter. Throughout the session, as the man who was the woman's husband and the girl's father related memories that they could relate to, they both laughed and cried. Throughout it all he kept reassuring them he was with God, and that he was happy.

He described his passing as "I was there, then I was here," and how it took everyone by surprise. It wasn't until he claimed responsibility for how it happened that I realized that he took his own life and I understood what happened.

What's memorable to me about that session is that when he pulled his energy away, Mary, the mother of Jesus, showed up, afterwards. 'Tell her I'm taking care of my son,' she said.

"Are you Catholic?" I asked. The daughter said that she wasn't, but that her mother was. I asked her mother, "Do you have a strong devotion to our Blessed Mother?"

She nodded her head.

"Well, she came to me and wants me to tell you that she's heard your prayers. She wanted me to tell you, 'I'm taking care of *my* son.'"

When the man's wife heard this, she broke down and began to sob. "Every day I say a prayer to Mary, 'Please take care of *your* son.'"

Those on the Other Side, who put themselves there, aren't alone. The Eternal Light of Love sends everything, and everyone they need, to help them heal, and find the peace they couldn't find when they were here on earth.

Now, to answer the other part of your question. When I do a reading for someone, it's almost as though I'm in a daydream. The reason I say that is that when the session is over, and I "wake up," I quickly forget what was said, much the same way we forget dreams when we wake up from sleeping. The reason is because the messages weren't meant for me. I'm just the instrument the souls use to give them a human voice.

When I receive a question about the souls and the hereafter, sometimes I'll be reminded of something a soul or souls have said during readings I've done. Other times, I'll go for a walk, and ask God and the souls for an answer from *their* perspective. Sometimes I'll receive an answer, and other times I won't. Why? Because they say that there are some answers we cannot know because it would take away from the lessons we need to learn while we're here, and that they, and the Beautiful One, love us too much to do that to us.

What about Atheist Who Commit Suicide?

I was just reading one of your posts about reuniting with our loved ones in heaven and that they want us to know they are o.k. My heart hurt and I had the thought, "Yes, but the wait is so long. What if you don't believe in heaven… and what about suicides?"

Even if there is a heaven, isn't it believed that people who commit suicide don't go to heaven? (One of our mutual friends committed suicide, and even though Pete's death was ruled an accident, I have my suspicions it may have been a suicide.)

I hope that wherever your spirit is, Pete, that you are at peace.
Ellen

Dear Ellen,
I'm inferring from your questions that your friend Pete, didn't believe in "Heaven," before he apparently took his own life. Well, I have nothing but good news for you that I hope helps your heart feel better.

First, because there's no time in the hereafter, no matter how long it takes, when you're finally reunited with your loved ones in the hereafter, it'll appear that only a moment has passed since you last saw each other.

Secondly, life in the hereafter isn't contingent on whether someone believes in its existence. The love the Beautiful One has for us is unconditional. It's one of those things that the souls joyously tell us that we must experience for ourselves. Whether someone believes in God or not, God believes in them.

Finally, where Pete is, you will be, as well. Reunited in a place of peace, joy, love, serenity and understanding. And you'll see me too… wagging my finger at you saying, "I told you so!"

Depressed… Addicted… What Was His Life Review Like?

My son died of suicide, depressed, and addicted. What was his life review like? Was he instantly healed of those issues or does he have something to do before he finds peace? Is he okay now?

Kathy

Whenever I do a session in which a soul who crossed themselves over comes through, one of the first things they want to do is to assure their loved ones that they are at peace and in the presence of the Beautiful One. Whatever torment or turmoil that they were going through which caused them to do what they did no longer exists for them.

They go on to say that they've not been judged for what they did. They were understood. The Eternal Light of Love and the souls understand what drove them to do what they did. They understand that your son didn't want to die. He just wanted the agony that robbed him of the strength to go on living that he was feeling to end.

Contrary to what some religions teach, or have taught, your son was *not* condemned to hell for doing what he did. The souls say that struggling to find a way to live in a way that allowed them to function normally despite their mental and emotional torment was hell, and played a huge factor in their decision to end their life.

Based on what the souls have said to me before, he was taken to a place where he could reflect, and heal, from the anguish that he had endured and had thought there was no way out of. During this time and in this place, there is no one to get in his face, so to speak. His companions during this period will be small creatures such as birds, rabbits, kittens, puppies, cats, and dogs as well as other animals that are there to help the healing process by offering unconditional love to souls such as your son.

Only when he is strong enough, will relatives, friends, and guides appear to help him understand and learn what he needs to know to continue his spiritual journey. Christ also appears, not as a judge, but as a consoler.

The souls have told me over and over again that suicide is a mistake on the part of those who have ended their time here in this way. It's a blunder they committed in their confusion. Even so, they take complete responsibility for what they've done and insist that even though they take complete responsibility for what they did and the pain they left behind, they were not made to feel guilty, and there's nothing for those they left here on earth to feel guilty about either.

Finally, your son would want you to know that you *will be reunited with him* on the Other Side, when you've learned the lessons you're here to learn, and not look at suicide as a way speed up the reunion. Until then, he will continue to be with you as your "guardian angel," never abandoning you, always there for you whenever you need him.

As far as his life review, based on what I've heard, he might have seen that he was loved more than he thought he was, and had options he wasn't aware of. He would also have become aware of the lessons he came here to learn, but didn't, and what he must do now not only to learn those lessons there, but repair the havoc and pain he caused when he took his own life. Not that any of this is a punishment from the Eternal Light of Love. It's a result being allowed to reflect, and heal so he can continue his spiritual journey on the Other Side to more fully experience the peace, love and joy of the Beautiful One who created him.

Love Is a Two-Way Street

Hey Anthony, I hope you don't mind me asking you a question. I had a tough morning (trigger) about Adam's suicide. So, I got to thinking and had a question I hope that you can help me with.

I've been thinking lately that I just wait for signs from Adam but I don't much in trying to connect with him. How can I nurture that relationship with him over there while I'm still here? How can I feel more engage with him spiritually?

I know that he's still with me because of my session with you. I hope that this makes sense.

Summer

Hi Summer,

I'm so happy that you know he's still with you. That's the entire purpose of a session. The souls want us to know that we're never alone.

I'm also delighted to hear that you're getting to the point where you're realizing that even communication with the souls is a two-way street! I cannot tell you how many times I've heard requests from the souls that their loved ones "stay in touch," by talking to them.

How do you do this? The same way you do with those you love who are still here on the earth. You talk to them. You share with them what is going on in your life. Yes, they already know, but they want to hear it from you.

I can't tell you how many times someone has asked me to tell their loved ones, who came through during their session, "I love you."

My response is *always*, "You just did."

Your brother wants you to know that every time you think of him, he's drawn to come to you from where he is. But that doesn't mean you're holding him back. To them it's a "spiritual hug."

Light a candle for him. Say a prayer. And reminisce about the great times you shared together. For them, these acts on your part are like spiritual boosters helping him in his journey in the hereafter while he's helping you with yours here.

Is He Still Angry at Me?

My husband committed suicide almost two years ago. I fought hard for him before he passed as he was suffering from what we now believe to be PTSD, that occurred from Army deployments.

The two months before he passed away were excruciating on me. The day before and the day after were the worst. He blamed me for things I didn't do, made threats to kill me, and almost sounded demonic over the phone.

I begged and pleaded for him to get help. I told him I only ever loved him. Still, his final texts to me were asking me to give our children money after he was gone, and his last text was good-bye, and "fuck you."

A few days after he died I felt compelled to get a memorial tattoo. It was an eight-hour session and during that time the artist informed me that he was also a medium. He explained that my husband was coming across still very arrogant and restless. He also detailed things that happened that were coming through that led to my husband's death.

I was left devastated and although I've grieved and asked all the "why" questions, I'm still unsure of what they medium had said, or how my husband feels for me now.

My question is, how can I know if he's at peace after this amount of earthly time has passed? There are moments I think I can feel him but I question everything. I don't want to keep feeling that he is still angry, because up until 3 or 4 months before he passed we were very happy.

Thank you for your time.

Tonya

Dear Tonya,

I'm familiar with PTSD as one of my brothers, who also served in the Army, has been diagnosed with the condition, and I was also diagnosed as possibly suffering from it as well. Post-traumatic stress disorder is a fairly new name for an old syndrome. Some of its symptoms are anxiety, depression, and physical illness because of being exposed to situations in which the difference between living or dying was as random as a roll of the dice.

It's a disease that doesn't show up on an x-ray, or CAT scan, but it's just as real as any physical disease and it's a nightmare that those who suffer from it cannot wake up from. Many of those who suffer from this illness look to numb the pain with alcohol, by abusing drugs or, as your husband did, ending their own lives.

Having done as many sessions as I have listening to the souls, and relaying their messages, I can tell you that if he really was coming to you through the artist whom you were getting your tattoo from, he would have told you that where he is now, he's healing from the emotional and mental anguish he was going through. That he finally found the peace he so desperately wanted and needed, but couldn't find while he was here.

You mentioned that three or four months before he crossed himself over, you two were very happy, which is confusing when you consider his behavior towards you near the end of his life. I'd like to suggest that his texts to you were acts of love, not anger. He expressed concern for his children, and I believe his final texts were because he knew he was going to end his life, and he wanted to make you believe he was angry with you so that you'd be angry at him. Now that he's on the Other Side, I'm sure he sees that all he did was hurt you, and will do everything within his power from where he is to make that up to you, and your children.

How can you know that he's at peace where he is? According to the souls, in the hereafter, peace, and love are the rule, not the exception. There isn't anyone condemning him for what he did, or the way he behaved towards you in the end. There's only understanding, not only from the other souls who are there, but from the Eternal Light of Love, as well. It's that empathy that allows him to heal.

You also mentioned "feeling" him, but questioning everything. That "feeling" is him trying to tell you that his love for you is still alive, and that he's still with you, watching over you, and your children.

If you're going to question *anything*, you should be questioning if the artist who did your memorial tattoo was really a medium. In my never to be humble opinion, based on how you felt walking away from what you heard, the answer is "no."

What if Suicide is the Only Option?

I am very interested in a reading, but I would like to ask you a question or two. Do you do the reading yourself or is it computer generated? I do not mean to offend you but there are people out there who are less than honest.

Second question, what if someone came to you and beyond a shadow of a doubt showed you that suicide was the best if not the only way to deal with their situation. This is only a hypothetical situation but if it were true, would you help them cross over?

This has nothing to do with the reading I want, it's to see if I'm dealing with you or a computer, and again I apologize if I have offended you. I look forward to your response.

Name withheld

While I'm not at all offended by your question, I must admit that I've never heard of a "computer-generated" medium reading. I know that they're done with numerology and astrology, but I'm not even sure how one involving messages from souls of your loved ones could even be done. I guess that someone could read a New Age book about how the souls are at peace, and program that into a computer, but messages coming from the souls in a session with a *legitimate* medium are extremely personal. I always tell the people I'm doing readings for that what's being communicated won't make sense to me because they're not supposed to. They're meant for the people receiving them. I'm only the messenger.

I had to read your question more than once to make sure I understood what you're asking and that I'm answering your question as best as I can. It seems to me that ultimately, you're asking me if it's okay for you to kill yourself. Or if the souls on the Other Side would give permission to someone who comes to me who has lost the hope and strength to carry on to do so.

As I said before, during a session, I'm only the messenger. My job is to give the souls a human voice, and I can tell you this – I've never heard a soul say to their loved ones it was a good example to follow. In fact, in all the sessions I've done, the souls have done the opposite, discouraging their loved ones from doing the same thing they did.

While they say it's not the unforgivable sin that many religions proclaim it to be, at the same time they say that it's not the best, or only solution, no matter how bleak things may seem.

Why?

Because when they do their life review they see that there were options and solutions that they couldn't see in the state of mind they were in but would have seen if they had hung in there a bit longer. Given time, they realized that the outcome could have been different. That there was a lesson in all the turmoil that they were going through that they would have benefitted from here, and in the hereafter, and their tears would have turned into triumph.

A grain of wheat faces one of three futures. It might be placed in a sack, and dumped into a stall where it's fed to swine. It might be ground into flour and made into bread. Or it might be placed into the ground and produced a thousand grains like itself.

A seed sprouts and grows in the darkness of soil.

Our growth happens in the darkness of our despair, failures, ignorance and feelings of helplessness.

What do the souls suggest that we do? Especially those who took their own lives?

Whatever we can to find hope in the situation we find ourselves in, and to hold on to that courage with all the strength we can muster. They say that everything happens for a reason, and contains a lesson that will help us grow in love for others and ourselves that we can grow from. We must do anything and everything necessary to hang on long enough so that whatever we're going through will pass; and it will.

A grain of wheat has no say over its future. You do.

The time will come when we will all leave the earth and return to where we truly belong. If you're speaking of yourself in your *hypothetical* question, the souls of your loved ones would encourage you to do the best you can to get through each day you wake up, even if you can do so by the skin of your teeth. The suffering you're going through now will be a distant memory, but the rewards, the joy and peace you'll experience having benefited from the lesson you've learn by having gone through it, will far surpass your wildest imaginings.

Why Shouldn't I Commit Suicide?

Hi Anthony,

If you've never done a reading during which a soul expressed regret for choosing to self-deliverance, then why would they say that lessons are easier learned here? Isn't this three dimensional plane the worst for experiencing physical and emotional pain? The mental and emotional trauma can be excruciatingly paralyzing.

Also, quoting you, "For these precious souls, however, they just don't seem to be able to do that. I don't think it's because of a weakness in their character. In fact, it may be just the opposite... they may be just too good for this world. Whatever the reason, they can't develop the protective barrier around themselves that they need to withstand the trials and tribulations we must all face during our life here. When this happens, they choose to learn the lessons they need in a world of peace."

This is definitely me!!! You wouldn't believe the protection I have tried to embrace myself in. Being a mental and emotional nerve ending doesn't make for a great successful journey through this life. Debilitating is debilitating. Would the world of peace you are talking about be "the other side?"

Then so be it, no?

Mike

Dear Mike,

There is a reason that you're still here, and still breathing. It's not your time to leave. You still have work to do, and lessons to learn.

I've heard the souls say to the souls of their loved ones that *everything* happens for a reason, and it's all necessary to our journey while we're here on earth. But there is a catch – we not only have to live through it, and experience it, but we're supposed to learn from it. If we don't, then there isn't a reward for having gone through it either here, or in the hereafter.

What's important to remember is that no matter how much pain you're in, or how bumpy the road you've traveled, the question to ask isn't "Why?" but "What?"

"What is it I'm supposed to be learning from what's going on here that will benefit me in the hereafter?"

The souls say that they can't answer that question because part of our journey is to figure that out on our own, but they do say that it starts with believing in yourself. And remembering, *life can be better than it is now.*

Some of the most compassionate messages I've heard in readings come from the souls who themselves have lived here on the earth with mental and emotional issues. They know what it's like to live life in a cloud of fear, pain and uncertainty, and how it can enclose someone to the point that they feel that there is no way out of the turmoil they're in. So, when they tell their loved ones that everything they suffered during their time here on earth is rewarded to the point that they would gladly go through it all again to receive a fraction of the joy, peace, love and beauty that makes up their existence in the hereafter, they do so hoping to give us hope in our own suffering.

They insist that a life of beauty beyond our comprehension must be earned. We "earn" it by doing learning the lessons we came here to learn, and part of that means suffering, and going through the pain of loss. Our purpose is to create Heaven here on earth, and according to the souls, our worst and most trying experiences are designed to enable us to best learn how to do that.

Finding the strength to bring peace and hope to others, and a way to keep our own faith and hope intact despite our own pain is the *most* important lesson we learn while we're here. It's also the one thing that brings the most reward when we return to our eternal home.

Why? Because your example benefits others here, and the souls who are awaiting your return, in ways that you'll never know, until that day comes when you return to a world of joy.

I hope that you can find the strength, and the faith, to know that no pain lasts 100 years. One day, and it's only a matter of time, you'll see your loved ones again in an existence of peace, love and joy. Once you're there, it'll be difficult for you to even remember the pain that you're going through now, and the reward you receive will make every second you hurt something that you'd do all over again.

Mental Illness

Just going over one of two questions that I've asked you and forgot to ask about something regarding poor mental health that leads to suicide. Is these soul's path towards completing the learning process in the presence of loving beings on the other side different?

Most psychics will mention that suicides result in getting pushed right back in to another body and forced to relive their soul path, and it's supposed to be harder. Talk about two steps forward and one step back. Ever hear anything like this Anthony?

Mike

What we refer to as a mental illness, such as depression, the souls refer to as a *sickness of the heart*. The first couple of times I heard that I thought, *what an interesting way to put it*. The more I heard it and thought about it, the more I realized how accurate a description it was.

I used to believe that no one wakes up one morning, and thinks to themselves, "I'm going to kill myself today." Then I found out my friend Teri had been planning to do so for weeks, even marking the day she would do it on her calendar with a heart.

We all face problems here on earth, but sometimes, mental turmoil can be as fatal as cancer.

The word suicide may be used on someone's death certificate, but it doesn't begin to address what kind of nightmares might have been going on in their mind. Can depression and anxiety kill someone? You'd better believe it. Talk about living a life that feels as though every step they take is like walking on broken glass. That's why I've never heard a soul express regret over what they did, any more than I've heard one say that they regretted passing from any other disease.

What the souls who have done this want you to know is that if you're feeling this way, it's a lie. You have value. You are loved. You do matter.

The lie that you are worthless and unlovable can only exist when you isolate yourself from those who love you. Talk about how you're feeling. Reach out, listen to, and trust the voices of those who love you. Know that no matter what the lie tells you, if you bring it out into the open, you'll see it for what it really is.

The Beautiful One and the souls asked me to write this book because they want you to know the truth: *YOU are important.*

They want me to tell you not to believe the lie. Reach out. Pursue help. Get treatment.

Suicide doesn't end the pain. It only passes it on to others.

The souls insist that committing suicide is a mistake. The Eternal Light of Love understands this, so the idea that souls are "pushed back" here to relive their path, and hopefully "get it right" this time, is absurd.

Is the learning process for those who cross themselves over different? Keep in mind what the souls say — that everything that happens to us while we're here does so for a reason. They also say that what makes no sense now will when we go through our "life review" on the Other Side. We'll see the whys and wherefores with such clarity we'll find ourselves saying, "Of course it had to happen the way it did!"

Many of the souls who take responsibility for their passing, during readings I've done, have said that even before doing their life review they understood that if they'd just held out a little bit longer, whatever was going on with them would have worked itself out. That's why they encourage those they left behind to stay here and hang on with whatever hope that they can muster.

As far as their "learning curve" being different, those who hang in there until the bitter end, learning the lessons they came here to learn, and teaching the lessons they came here to teach, are immediately rewarded. For those who end their lives prematurely, whatever the lessons were that they didn't learn here, they say that they now must complete on the Other Side. Why? So that they can continue their spiritual growth. and experience even more deeply the presence, and love, of the Beautiful One, which is why, they also say, we all chose to come here to this spiritual cesspool in the first place.

Is Suicide a Life Plan?

From what I've read, you say that you've never heard from a soul who took responsibility for ending its own life express regret over what it had done. Yet, you also say that souls discourage their loved ones from doing the same thing, saying that what they did was a mistake. Is it because suicide is not part of any soul's plan for when they incarnate in the first place?

Mike

A woman named Debbie booked an appointment to see me. Even though she paid for a medium session, she wasn't sure that's what she needed. "I just felt compelled to call you. I don't know why, but it was like the spirits wanted me to talk to you." The last time I had seen her was probably three years before. Since that time, she had divorced a man who was mentally and emotionally abusing her, telling her she wasn't lovable which, unfortunately, she believed. She told me that since her divorce she had tried to take her own life twice in two weeks. The first time she was saved, ironically enough, by her ex-husband. The second time she told me that she knew God was telling her that this wasn't the right thing to do, so she took steps to get help after she took an overdose of pills. Since she didn't book an appointment to help her with her grief over losing someone she had loved, I felt the souls wanted me to help her deal with her distress over being alive. I shared with her a little of what the souls have told me about suicide, and I thought I'd share the same with you in this post.

Whenever someone comes across who has taken his own life, one of the ways I know is that his energy is as heavy at it gets. After doing many readings in which victims of suicide come through, I've come to understand that suicide is a disease that slowly erodes the person's will to live. For most of us, when we experience times that make us question how much more we can take, we respond by developing ways of coping until the pain passes or we overcome whatever obstacles are in our way. For these precious souls however, they just don't seem to be able to do that. I don't think it's because of a weakness in their character. In fact, it may be the opposite . . . they may just be too good for this world. Whatever the reason, they can't develop the protective barrier around themselves that they need to withstand the trials and tribulations we must all face during our life here. When this happens, they choose to learn the lessons they need in a world of peace.

I have never had a soul that chose this route say that it regretted its decision, but every one of them cautioned their loved ones against doing the same. Why? Because the lessons are so much easier to learn here.

Debbie wanted to take her own life because she felt unlovable. She married a man who constantly reinforced this belief. The lesson she was probably meant to learn is that she is lovable. She was created by the Eternal Light of Love who finds her impossible not to love, especially in her darkest moments. If she were successful in either one of her attempts, she would still have to learn why she's lovable, ironically, in an environment in which she is surrounded and supported by God's love. In other words, she'll find herself overwhelmed by love, not knowing why, because she crossed over not believing she was worthy of being loved. Not only that, but she'll have to learn why without the benefit of anyone getting in her face.

What I did with Debbie that night was to have her question whether she truly was unlovable. "I see you the same way God sees all of his children," I told her. "I see you as perfect, just the way you are. What's not to love?" I then helped her find all the reasons she is lovable. She left our appointment shining with joy and hope. "Besides," I told her, "You still have lessons to learn and to teach others." "How do you know?" she asked me. "You're still breathing."

■ ■ ■

After I responded to Mike's question, I received the following question from him -

So much for never meeting a soul who didn't "regret"" suicide, unless they don't, first, experience "regret" but otherwise know that it was still yet a mistake, because suicide is not part of any soul's plan for when they incarnate in the first place?

I just looked up the definition of "mistake" on Dictonary.com, and here's how it defines the word – *an error in action, calculation, opinion, or judgment caused by poor reasoning carelessness, insufficient knowledge, etc.*

There's one thing the souls talk about being able to benefit from that we can't now, and that's how, hindsight being 20/20, they can see the whole story of their lives and how it all made sense.

It's true, in all the session I've done in which a soul that crossed themselves over comes through, I've not heard of one who said that they regretted doing what they did. By the same token, I've been at the bedside of more people who were dying than I can remember, and they've never talked about regretting what they did in their lives, either. They did talk about regretting what they didn't do.

My father didn't finish high school. He dropped out to join the military, some many young men from Guam were doing at the time. He served in the Korean war, and the Vietnam war, as well. He was a genuinely brilliant man, but he knew that his lack of formal education was keeping him from going as far as he could go in in the Navy.

He attended night classes, and eventually earned his G.E.D. Afterwards, he quickly rose up the ranks, ending his 22-year career as a Chief Petty Officer. He knows that had he stayed in school to begin with, and beyond, he could have very well been an Naval Officer.

The souls compare suicide to dropping out of school. Saying that suicide is part of someone's life plan makes as much sense as a child entering kindergarten planning on dropping out of high school.

We come here to learn the lessons that will allow us to experience more deeply the Eternal Light of Love. These lessons are learned more easily here because of the trials and tribulations of this life. The souls say that *all* suffering we endure here is richly rewarded, earns us a higher place, and more joy, in the hereafter, if we can just hold on.

Again, as I've said before, while I've never heard a soul say that they "regretted" what they did, they've also said that they saw in their life review that if they could have hung in there a little longer, there were options available that they couldn't see at the time. Which is why they've also advised their loved one to hold on as long as they can. That should speak volumes as to their attitude towards suicide.

Do You Really Believe That?

I was reading what you wrote about Debbie on your blog. Do you really believe that? If you do, then can you tell me why God didn't save my friend from committing suicide?

Donna

I remember doing a reading several years ago for a woman whose mother crossed over when she was very young. During the session, her mother showed me her daughter hiding behind a cross.

When I mentioned this to the woman she said, "Well, I'm okay with her dying. Jesus needed my mother more than I did."

"Do you really think that the Eternal Light of Love is the Angel of Death?" I asked her. "Do you think God was so bored one day he thought to himself, 'Hmmm... I'm so bored I think I'll ruin this seven-year-old girl's life by taking her mother?'"

She sat there stunned for a moment and suddenly a flood of tears she'd been keeping in for more than 40 years came rushing out.

The Beautiful One doesn't take joy in watching us suffer, but allows us to go through it for our greater good, our spiritual growth, and for the rewards we earn for having gone through it. According to the souls when we come here we *know* that we're going to go through turmoil, and yet we decide to come here anyway. They say that we do so because we know that every second of pain, every struggle and every second of we spend making life better not only for ourselves, but others here on the earth, will pay off handsomely when they return home to the Eternal Light of Love.

They also say that we develop amnesia regarding all the plans we made before we came here, because knowing in advance what the lessons are that we'll learn will take away the need to learn them in the first place.

It's only natural that when we're knee deep in alligators, we forget that we're here to drain the swamp. I don't know about you but if I stub my big toe, the last thing I'm thinking about are all the starving children in Darfur. But that's the lesson of love – to remember others who are in pain while we're in the midst of our own. To try to make other's lives better while we're trying to better our own.

For some of us, the pain becomes so great that this lesson is lost in the midst of just trying to justify taking another breath, let alone going through another day. But the Beautiful One loves us too much to cut our lessons short by ending our suffering before learning the lesson it contains. Doing so would cut short the rewards we'll reap when we come back home to the Other Side.

What God does do is give us a chance to try again… and again, in the form of another breath, another sunrise, a smile or phone call from a loved one, another person with a listening ear, a counselor or an EMT. But when we get to the point that the desire for the pain to end exceeds our will to live, the Eternal Light of Love understands that too.

According to the souls I've heard who have taken their own lives, they see that if they had only hung in there a little longer, they would have realized that they had options they didn't know that they had. People that God was putting in their lives to try to help ease their pain.

Didn't She Suffer Enough?

Dear Mr. Quinata,

I am a 67-year-old woman who has lost her youngest daughter of 31 years to suicide. She was a very intelligent and loving person. She had a lot of mental problems which didn't improve with treatment. She wanted to live very much but her problems overcame her. I am devastated and feel a terrible sense of loss.

I have bought your book – We Are Never Alone. I find it very difficult because of my mental turmoil. I shall be highly obliged if you would answer the following questions for me:

Will she suffer because she committed suicide? I have read that people who commit suicide go to darker levels in the spirit world. She has already suffered so much that it breaks my heart to think that she will again suffer.

I have read that when people reincarnate, a part of their soul always remains in the spirit world so that they are always available there. Will I get to meet my daughter when I cross over?

I am a middle class Indian and cannot afford to come to the USA for a reading. Also, though I can write English well, I find it difficult to understand English as spoken by you. That is the reason I am writing to you.

Thank you and hoping to hear from you,
With love and regards,
Lakshmi

Dear Lakshmi,

It tears at my heart when I receive as letter such as this one, but I'm always grateful because it gives me a chance to set the record straight. You're in more than enough pain losing your daughter, and for them to add to your distress.... Why they do this is beyond me, but that's why the souls are so vocal about this subject.

Is your daughter suffering in a "darker" level because of what she did? The souls say that after they go through their life review they do place themselves in a "level" that reflects what they've learned and what they need to learn, but not to think of it as being like "floors" in a building. It's more like grade levels in school.

Another way it was explained to me was to think of souls as being like containers of liquid. A container might be as small as a tumbler, or as large are as 55-gallon drum. If you fill them with liquid, both are full, but one contains more than the other.

It's much the same way with the souls.

Being in a lower level doesn't mean one is in a "darker" place, because no soul can ever not feel the love and light of the Beautiful One. It means that they have more lessons to learn to experience this light and love to an even greater degree.

When it's your time to return to the hereafter, I promise you that one of the souls you will meet will be your daughter. Better still, it will only seem like a second since you last saw her; and you'll find out that she's been with you all along, watching you, responding to your thoughts about her, and guiding and inspiring you while you were still here.

Your question reminded about reincarnation reminded me of a phone session I did in which a woman's father came through. I asked her if her father was a physicist. She said yes. I told her that the reason I was wondering was that he wanted her to know that he was spending a lot of time with his "hero," Albert Einstein!

After her father pulled his energy away she told me that she talked to another medium who told her that her father had already reincarnated, and was five years old at the time they spoke. This worried her because she thought that she wouldn't see her father again when it was her time to cross over.

The souls have told me that reincarnation does happen, but typically after a long time spent in the hereafter, and the decision to return is a carefully thought out one. But they also say that much of the joy they experience is being with their loved ones in an existence of beauty and peace, free of pain and tears.

Don't worry. You won't find yourself there, asking to see your daughter only to have a soul snap their fingers and say, "She just left 30 minutes ago to go back to the earth."

By the way, you do not need to see a medium to know your daughter is okay. Just talk to her. Pray for her. Light a candle for her. I don't care what anyone says otherwise, your daughter is safely in the company of souls who understand why she did what she did, and in the arms of the Eternal Light of Love.

Will I See My Daughter Again?

Dear Anthony,

I have read that some children remember their past life which they lived just 10 or 20 years. So how will their loved ones meet them when they cross over?

Another subject unrelated to the above which agonizes me is that Edgar Cayce thinks that suicide is a terrible sin (might be I misunderstood what was written because it is difficult to grasp the meaning of what he says).

Since I am personally affected (my daughter took her own life) and am living in the hope that I will meet my daughter when my time comes and that she is happy and peaceful, the above-mentioned things unsettle me.

Please enlighten me.
With love and prayers,
Lakshmi

Hi, Lakshmi!

Thank you for writing and asking these extremely important questions!

It is true that some children will remember "past lives" from a lived supposedly lived just a few years before, but my understanding from the souls is that is extremely rare. What is typical is that someone who crosses over will choose to stay on the Other Side waiting for their loved ones to reunite with them and guiding them while they do so. According to the souls, the decision to return here to the earth may take years (I'm talking hundreds of years) to do so because they know how hard it is here. I've even heard some souls say, "It's just too hard there. I'm never going back. I'll stay here and learn what I need to learn even though it takes longer to do so."

However, there, as here, the souls have "free will," and some will choose to return here after only a brief stay there. If that is the case, there's no need to worry because whoever they loved and were connected to in their previous incarnation, they are still connected to even though they've returned here to the Earth. Keep in mind, death is not the end of life, love or relationships. We come here for one reason, and one reason, only – to learn lessons that will enable us to grow spiritually. Once we learn those lessons, we return home taking the lessons of love we learned with us. And we return to our loved ones both in this life and our previous lives. We never lose them.

Is suicide a "sin?" It is when you consider the original meaning of the word. It's not my intent to bring religion into this, but the Biblical word which is translated as "sin" is from the Hebrew word, hata. It was an archery term and literally refer to missing the "gold" at the center of a target.

We come here to learn a lesson, and we return when we've fully learned that lesson, and have taught all the lessons we've come here to teach. The act of taking our own life before we've learned that lesson implies that we've missed the "bull's eye," or the reason we came here was, to begin with. Every soul I've heard from says that they don't regret what they did, but do not recommend that anyone follows their example.

Is this because they're in some dark place of isolation and torment? No. In fact, they've all said that God holds them close because of what they went through that would cause them to make that decision in the first place. But was does happen is that the lesson they came here to learn must still be learned there if they are to grow and enjoy the presence of the Eternal Light of Love even more.

You will see your daughter again. That much I promise. She is happy and at peace. That I guarantee. If anyone tells you otherwise, put your fingers in your ears, hum loudly, and walk away.

If you read any book that makes you fearful for your daughter, use it to start a fire. Your daughter would want you to be at peace knowing that she's okay, she's loved and continuing her spiritual journey in a place of peace. But every soul who has crossed themselves over has been unanimous in saying that what they did was a mistake.

I Hurt Him… More Than I Knew

Hello Anthony,

Long story short, I've lived a tragic story. Most recently, my boyfriend… who I just broke up with, not only committed suicide but took his young daughter's life as well. Right now, I am dealing with guilt. He tried, reaching out to me and I didn't have it in me to respond back. Perhaps you could help me find a way to say sorry.

I didn't break up with him because I didn't love him. I did, very much so. We were connected on a different level. I broke up with him because I had my own things I needed to work on before we could be anything. I just wanted to be able to give him my all. In doing so, I hurt him… more than I knew.

As I am writing this, this is all very fresh. It's on the new… it's only been 4 days.

Thank you for taking the time to read this, I only wish I had the capability of what you do. A definite gift.

(Name withheld to protect privacy)

First, I want to offer you my condolences and prayers.

The souls often refer to suicide as "self-murder." While that sounds harsh, their point is to let those who remain behind is that they're not to blame. They also say that those who cross themselves over aren't held responsible because depression is to the soul what cancer is to the body.

Souls don't come to me without a good reason, such as someone here needing to hear from them. Having said that, without hearing from your friend, I can only guess that his pain was so great that he thought he was sparing his daughter from the same heartache he was feeling.

Several years ago, I did a reading for a mother and her daughter. Their son, and brother, came through and during the session and I found out that he took the life of his girlfriend and two daughters, before taking his own life. I thought to myself, "If anyone deserves to be in hell, it's this guy."

If you've read my books, you know that the souls there's no such thing as "hell." Still, to be honest, I was stunned to be told to tell them that all of them were together on the Other Side! That's the beauty of the afterlife.

Based on all the readings I've done during which someone who crossed themselves over, or whose life was taken by another, I can tell you that they would want you to know that they are fine, and are working hard from where they are to help you be okay. They'd want you to continue to take care of yourself and know that when your time comes you will see them again in a place of light, love, and peace.

I will remember you, and them, in my daily prayers.

What Do the Souls say about Assisted Suicide?

Anthony,
What do the souls say about assisted suicide? I'm asking because when a pet we love is suffering, it's considered humane to "put it to sleep."
Can't the same be said for helping those we love who are suffering?

Marianne

There's a story about what a child had to say after his dog was euthanized. "Everyone is born to learn how to live a good life – like loving everyone and being nice, right? Well, animals already know how to do that, so they don't have to stay as long."

Whether the story is true or not, the message is a great one. The main purpose for us to come into this plane of existence is to go through a spiritual crash course in love so that we can rise to a higher level in the hereafter. According to the souls, pets are gifts to us from the Beautiful One to help us learn those lessons. They are one of the greatest gifts given to us by the Eternal Light of Love.

We, on the other hand, come to here with a plan that outlines our life's work for the time that we're here. Our efforts are not only for the benefit our spiritual growth but those whose lives we impact and influence, and there are lessons to be learned not only by us, but by those who love us, in our suffering.

According to the souls, whatever we came here to do that is not finished must be finished in the hereafter. There is only one way to build a world of peace, joy and happiness for ourselves in the world that awaits us, and that is to build it here, brick by brick, struggle by struggle, act of love and compassion by acts of love and compassion.

None of the struggles we experience here are easy by any stretch of the imagination but, according to the souls, all of them are necessary. What we're going through, and watch those we love going through may not make sense now, but they say it will make *perfect* sense when complete our journey and return to the hereafter.

The Beautiful One loves us too much to cut short any of our lessons by ending our turmoil, no matter how painful they are while we're going through it because the rewards for doing so are so great.

The souls say that the chaos, struggles, and suffering we go through in this life earn us the right to live in a world that is free of all of that. They beg us to stick to the plan we made for ourselves before we came here, to see it through, learn what we can, and that we allow those we love to do the same.

I'm Losing the Will to Live

Dear Anthony,

I went through your blog in the past day and read all your posts regarding suicide. I don't know if you'll ever get this email or if you'll even read all of it, I don't blame you if you don't. The reason I am coming to you is because I am in a lot of emotional pain and have no idea where to go for answers. I am at the lowest point in my life. I've been struggling with depression for over 6 years, I'm 20 years old and I don't want to live. I am in so much pain constantly that I can't bear it. As the years have passed I've seen myself deteriorate and get more and more depressed. The reason I never killed myself was because I was scared of going to 'hell'.

But a year ago I started reading a few different medium's blogs and after reading about all their similar perceptions, I understood the general idea of the afterlife. Religion never made sense to me but what I was reading in these blogs really clicked for me. I felt a huge lift off my shoulders and I was no longer afraid to die. So, I began to plan my suicide and a few months later attempted it. I made a mistake and was found before it was too late.

It's been 6 months later and I am still in the same place, if not worse. I tried to find some hope to hang on to for a short while, for my family because I don't want them to suffer. So, I tried to pick my life up and get help and get out there and become a functional person again. But that fell apart very quickly and left me worse than I was because no matter what I do, my depression always gets the better of me. I was foolish for thinking I could start living life again. I am just in too much pain. I can't do it. I have no will to live. I am always so sad, so miserable.

I can't sleep at night anymore, no matter how hard I try. I just lay awake and cry.

I always feel out of place no matter where I go and what I do. I never feel like I fit. I always feel so worthless. I compare myself to everyone I see. I never feel good enough for this world. I feel so ugly I can barely look in the mirror because I am disgusted with myself. I have so many flaws and I can't fix them all and I can't stand it.

I have so much self-hatred, I don't want to be me anymore. I don't want to be this person anymore. I don't want to live this life and I don't want to feel this pain anymore.

I'm writing to you because I believe it is my fate to commit suicide. I've read that we have spirit guides and guardian angels to guide and help us. I try so hard to look for signs from them so I can know what to do, but I feel so alone, even spiritually. I even look to see signs from deceased loved ones but there's never anything. I just want to know if I should let go. If I should kill myself. I know how grim that sounds and I know that in your posts you say that nobody should ever kill themselves, but what would you suggest to somebody who is in so much pain and can't get out of it?

Who's been like this for years and nothing seems to work?

Should I just continue in severe depression just for the sake of living?

Should I live for the next ten years completely miserable?

It doesn't make any sense to me. If God and the spirits could see how much pain I'm in, wouldn't they want me to let go? What's the alternative? Letting me live like this until I die naturally?

I don't know what else to do. I believe it is my fate to commit suicide. If it wasn't, my spirit guides would have told me not to do it by now. If it wasn't, wouldn't something good have happened in my life by now to make things at least a tiny bit better?

Things just stay the exact same. It's like a cycle and me ending my life would be the only way to break it. I just want to hear something that makes sense. I just want to hear that it's okay to do it. That God and the spirits understand.

I also have a bit of a drug problem as well. I am a heroin user. Over the weekend, I got high as I usually do, and ended up overdosing. I had no idea what happened, I don't remember anything, I just blinked and woke up to police officers and EMTs everywhere and my family hysterical. They said I stopped breathing and my heart stopped and that I was turning blue. Somehow, I survived. But I did spend the night in a hospital. It got me thinking though, this seems to be my second close call with death and I escaped both times. I feel like maybe God doesn't want me dead for some reason. I'm not sure why. I don't feel like I have much purpose here so I'm not sure why I'm meant to be here if that's the case.

I want to ask you a question, it's okay if you don't know the answer. I feel very alone spiritually. This weekend got me thinking about that again. I feel like I never get any signs from spirit guides or anything of that sort. I always ask for it. I want some kind of dream, or just something that lets me know that someone is watching over me and just that there's someone or something there, that there's a reason for all this pain or if I'm really even meant to be alive or not. But I never get any sort of response in any way.

What I wanted to ask you was, why do you think that is?

Has everyone/thing in the afterlife given up on me?

Why has no one reached out?

Anna

Dear Anna,

One of the things I love about your e-mail to me is that you ask the questions so many people have, in such a way that more people than either you or I will ever know until we enter the hereafter, will benefit from you asking. So, I'm going to break down my answer into a couple of different parts and hopefully it will give you the help and assurance you're looking for.

Signs

I can tell you that the Eternal Light of Love and the souls are constantly reaching out and speaking to you, as they do to *all* of us, but not every "sign" from those in the hereafter is going to be dramatic, or even mystical. It might be a kind word or gesture from a stranger when you feel most alone. Something you're worried about resolves itself with seemingly on its own, or with very little effort on your part. It might be receiving an answer to an email that you sent to a medium, when you weren't really expecting one. Or "blinking" and waking up to police officers, EMTs and family surrounding you and worried that you were going to die.

Signs from the Beautiful One and the souls always point to the same thing - that you are not alone, you are loved and you are cared for. You have more of a connection than you realize, and the souls are walking with you, and watching over you, caring for your well-being while you're here, even if you can't feel this to be the truth. But if you take the time to really look at the events happening in your life, you'll see that you've been given signs all along, although they may be subtle and easy to reject.

In other words, you don't recognize the signs you've been given because you don't know how to look at them. Rather than demanding that they come to you in a dream (which happens more often than people realize), ask them to help you see, feel, and hear, the messages that they've been sending you from the moment your journey here on the earth began.

I would say that you probably need to pay closer attention and be a bit more open to the possibility that you already are receiving signs from the souls who are trying to encourage you to continue this journey you're on while you're still here. They won't give you a sign that they know you can't handle, so don't expect anything dramatic. Start by accepting, without any doubt that you are loved by the souls on the Other Side, and the Beautiful One in whose image and goodness you were created. If you can do that, then you'll see that they really have been speaking to you all along.

Suffering

I thought I'd share with you a letter that I wrote to my cousin Lisa, my sister Meridith, and my brother Edward -

I'm not writing this to you as your brother who adores you, and prays for you every day, but as a psychic medium whom the souls in the hereafter use to give them a human voice, so that they can give us hope while we are still here on the earth. After having done countless sessions during which I've listened to their wisdom, I know what they'd say to you right now, as you go through this period in your life.

They would tell you that everything you're going through, all your anguish, and all your pain, physically, mentally, and emotionally may not make sense right now, but it will.

They'd tell you that you're not alone. Everyone you've ever loved, and who loved you back, never dies. They've simply gone from this life to an even greater life of unspeakable peace, joy, and tranquility; where they are watching over you, standing by you, praying for you, loving you, and cheering you on. And you will see them again. That includes all your furry loved ones too.

They'd also tell you that everything you're going through is not unnoticed by the Divine Presence who loves you unconditionally. God doesn't enjoy seeing you in pain, but allows it so that you can grow spiritually from what you're enduring now. The souls also say that what awaits you for patiently persevering through it will make everything you're going through right now a distant memory. There is no pain, and there are no tears, on the Other Side.

I know it sounds crazy but the more you endure and overcome here, the more magnificent it will be for you there. So, they would tell you to hang in there. Don't give up. No pain lasts 100 years. When the time comes for you to return, the anguish you're going through now will no longer exist. Only love, peace and unimaginable joy will be your reality.

There have been people who have come to me as a medium wanting to know what awaits them when their time comes. One of them was a woman named Ann, who was diagnosed with Stage 4 breast cancer, and an atheist. I told her that there was a "surprise party" being held in her honor three weeks from the day I did her session for her. She told me that she had no idea what I was talking about. She crossed over 22 days later.

After she "changed her address," her sister booked a session with me, and during the reading Ann told me, "You didn't tell me how beautiful it is here!" I didn't, because I couldn't. There's no words that can describe what is waiting for us when it's our time to return home.

They would want you to know that the suffering you're going through isn't a punishment for anything you've done wrong. I'd like to share a story about a woman and a silversmith with you that goes like this —

A few ladies met to study the scriptures. While reading the third chapter of Malachi, they came upon a remarkable expression in the third verse:

"And He shall sit as a refiner and purifier of silver" (Malachi 3:3).

One lady told the others that she would visit a silversmith, and report to the others on what he said about the subject.

Without telling him the reason for her visit, she asked the silversmith to tell her about the process of refining silver. After he had fully described it to her, she asked, "Sir, do you sit while the work of refining is going on?"

"Oh, yes ma'am," the silversmith said. "I must sit and watch the furnace constantly. If the time necessary for refining is exceeded in the slightest degree, the silver will be injured."

The lady immediately understood the beauty and comfort of the expression, "He shall sit as a refiner and purifier of silver."

We come here to learn lessons, and teach lessons, in love, but sometimes these lessons can only be learned, and taught in the "fire" of suffering. But God is always watching, and helping us learn those lessons in the circumstances in our lives. Our trials do not come at random, and He will not let us be tested beyond what we can endure.

Before she left, the lady asked one final question, "How do you know when the process is complete?"

"When I can see my own image in the silver, the refining process is finished."

I look at the three of you and I can't help but think of God.

Personally speaking, I cannot tell you how each of you inspire me. Thank you for you being in my life, and a part of my family. I love you. I always have. I always will. And I celebrate you in my prayers.

Author's note – my cousin Lisa crossed shortly after I wrote this letter, and my brother Eddie returned to the Other Side just a few days ago (April 10, 2017).

EPILOGUE

When Anthony asked me to tell my story at first I was taken aback; how does one tell the story of losing your child? So, I asked him how I should tell the story and he told me to tell it from my heart. I read that and I cried. I cried for my lost daughter, for my wife and kids and all the people in my life that have been impacted by the loss. I cried for the other parents I've talked with that have lost children to suicide who bear the pain. And I know with one hundred percent surety that I will continue to cry, periodically and when I least expect it. Tears brought on by a song, a picture, a thought, a memory, her empty chair at the holiday table, her missing face at the family parties. So, there is a story to be told and Anthony was correct. It needs to be told from the heart.

Collie was the third daughter born to us and I was blessed to be her father. As she grew we realized she was an extremely sensitive child, quiet and shy but with a loving disposition, deep intellect and a mature nature. From my research and discussions with mediums she might be best described as an "old soul". As she approached her formative years we noticed she was not typical. She refused to wear dresses, makeup. She was not at all interested in the usual feminine interests. Undeterred by this I took her shopping and she dressed much like me. At some point, we knew she was gay but waited till she was ready to tell us herself. I can still remember her coming into the room as a teenager to have this serious talk with me to tell me she was gay. I think she was nervous how I'd react. I just smiled and told her I had figured it out long before and her mother and I loved her no matter what her preference. We just wanted her to be happy.

As she progressed into her teenage years she flourished, making friends, dating and was outstanding academically. She joined the Jr. ROTC and excelled. At this point we noted she had a strong math and artistic ability. Her freehand drawing was remarkable and we were amazed that she had such a strong combination of mathematical, intellectual and creative talents. She also had a sarcastic side like much like me and her sense of humor was priceless. We would take her and her girlfriend on vacations with us and I remember these times as some of the best of my life. No parent could ask for a better child. At this point she told us she was transgender and again we were completely supportive. She was our child and although I didn't understand, it didn't matter. We would love her and support her no matter what she wanted.

After high school, she was accepted into the engineering program at UMass Dartmouth and I remember how happy she was and how she flourished and made friends. She would come home on the weekends and I'd drive her back on Sundays. She and I would talk the whole ride about the family, her friends and her future. Everything seemed bright and well. It was a shock to us when she called us in tears from school. Her relationship with her girlfriend was apparently failing and she wanted to come home and try and repair it. Given her distraught state which was unlike her usual calm demeanor her mother and I drove her home from school that night and we discussed her concerns and offered her advice.

As the week progressed it became apparent that her long-term relationship was over but we encouraged never the less that at 19 she had her whole life ahead of her and there would be others. She told us she had talked to a doctor and wanted to begin the transition from female to male. We were fine with that and would work with her on what needed to be done. Everything seemed well, she seemed happy and although we felt her pain over the relationship we figured she'd bounce back. After all, who hasn't had a broken heart or two?

The last time I would see my precious daughter alive it was on the night of March 28, 2014. Her mother and I had just talked to her and she was optimistic. I remember I was in bed fiddling with my tablet. Her mother was asleep. Collie came into our outer room where the washer/dryer is located to do laundry. We looked at each other, made silly faces. I was comfortable she was ok. Later she would post on Facebook, *Just when u think it's getting better it gets 4000 times worse.*

Linda had woken up at 4:30 that morning, read it, and woke me up with a fright. Collie's door was locked but we had a key and opened it. She had hung herself on the crossbeam. I can remember screaming while

I tried to hold her up. I remember getting her down and her mother and I trying to resuscitate her. I remember covering her with a blanket and holding her head in my lap because she had a calm look on her face like she was sleeping.

Then the police, fire and ambulance showed up. They were professional and kind. Family arrived and people stood with us but much of this is a blur for me.

Then there was the funeral and burial to which there are no words to describe when it is your child. We cremated her because I could not put her in the ground. Through it all I realized a part of me had died as well.

I will never know exactly what happened that night. At that moment, someone sent her a message, probably on Snapchat, that was so hurtful it pushed her to an area she could not manage.

There was finality to her actions. She was afraid of the dark and had shut off her lights. She locked the door which she never did. We were right down the hall but she never reached out to us.

As a parent, as a father, I was there to nurture and protect my children but how do you protect them from themselves?

Now, we were left to carry on. The "new normal" we called it. The pain is like a wound that scars but doesn't heal. It is with you constantly as reminder and periodically enflames.

Through this process, my wife and I have learned a great deal. Family is not always blood and friends & family will sometimes disappoint.

Another notion I have heard is that, "God will never give you more than you can handle." I don't think that is incorrect. We are fallible beings in an imperfect world. He doesn't promise us a perfect life but He does offers us perfect love. When we are at our weakest, He will be at His strongest for us. Just think of the footprints in the sand because I have experienced this. If you look for Him He is there, not in a miraculous way, but in those he puts in your life. In my case, it was a friend who became a brother when he stood with me while I read her eulogy ready to step in if I faltered. And his mother and father that have since become surrogate parents for us.

I met a woman on the train who had suffered the devastating loss of her husband a year earlier in a car accident. We have since supported each other though anniversaries and holidays when loss for us is more keenly felt.

A Brother in a small chapel I had wondered into to light a candle noticed my pain and asked me if I was okay. I proceeded to fall apart and tell him my story. He held me while I cried.

After I regained some composure I remember saying I didn't know why I wandered in there. He looked at me, smiled, and said, "Do you think maybe you were supposed to?"

There have been many other times when I have had this type of intervention when I needed it. All I can say is trust in Him and look for it. It will be there.

I also believe unfalteringly that God is eternal love. I remember confronting Father Thomas before the sermon at Collie's funeral on the notion of suicide and Hell because I would have none of that. He calmed me down and told me that he had experienced suicide in his family and eased my concerns with his kindness and understanding. His sermon was eloquent and beautiful. I can still hear him saying he was sure Jesus met her at the gates of Heaven and held her close, telling her, "I'm sorry life was so hard for you."

I do not know the demons my daughter was tormented by but as a father who loves his children unconditionally how much more does the ultimate Father love us? I have not a doubt in my mind that she is safe in the eternal love of God's light, made whole and new again and free from pain.

I have been told her actions were "selfish" by some and I even had on person ask me how she did it. In many cases the intentions are good but most do not realize the extent of damage caused by suicide, It's even more enhanced by the loss of a child. So, when these comments come, and they will, it is best to forgive and not take them to heart.

My daughter's passing has been like a pebble in a pond whose ripples have impacted many lives. For myself, as I run down my current career and move closer to retirement I plan on starting a Master's program training as a "Marriage & Family Counselor."

I do not know the reason these things have happened but this feels right - something I'm supposed to do. I hope that through my experience if I can help a parent with grief, a child with their pain... if I can help one person not do what my daughter did... then I will have honored the memory of my daughter and will have lived a life worth living.

To the child or person contemplating this action I beg you to please reconsider. I cannot understand your pain but I guarantee you that you are not alone. You are loved. You are important. You matter.

I want to tell parents that you cannot hold your children close enough, love them enough, and watch them enough. And if we lose them they are always with us and never forgotten. We carry them in our hearts till we also are called home to be with them again.

Richard Cahill

ACKNOWLEDGEMENTS

Writing this book, I've proven the adage that, "Fools rush in where angels fear to tread." This was an extremely difficult project for me, for many different reasons. It took me more than a year to write it, and during that time I could feel the heaviness that the souls who crossed themselves over were feeling when they were still here on earth. It wore me out, but it also gave me the compassion I needed to do the best I could to convey their messages of hope in this book. And I would not have been able to finish it without help from those in the hereafter, but here on earth as well.

I want to thank the Beautiful One, and the souls, for supporting me and seeing me through this project. I hope that I've served you well, and that what I've written will bring comfort, hope and some peace to those who read your words.

I want to thank my sisters Meridith and Nadine, and my brothers Eddie and Steve, and their families, for their love and acceptance of who I am, and what I'm trying to do while I'm here. I love you more than words can say.

Thank you, Camille Massing, my dear friend, for all your support throughout my journey as a medium, and as a person. You have always shown me God and His love for me. I love you.

I also want to thank Marianne Shotto. I've watched you get knocked down, only to bounce back. Your fighting spirit is such an inspiration to me. I'm lucky to have you in my life, and to be able to call you my friend.

And you, my friend, Donna Nikolla, have a place in my heart and always will.

Thank you, Fred Vallongo. Your encouragement and support in writing this book meant more to me than you know.

I want to thank Andi, Amber, Debbie, Donna, Mair, Richard, and Summer, for sharing their stories with me, and allowing me to share them with you. And thank you Anna, Ellen, Kathi, Lakshmi, Mike, and Tonya, for your questions.

They've done so because they share my hope that by doing so the wall of silence that surrounds suicide will one day, slowly but surely, come down; and survivors will be able to talk about their loved ones with joy, and those who are in pain will be able to talk about how they're feeling, without shame.

I love you, and celebrate you in my prayers.

Dear Anthony,

I'm writing to thank you for my reading last Saturday. I felt an e-mail was insufficient considering what it meant to me.

It's taken a few days for me to process it and get back to some form of regular life. I'm sure I'll still go back to it over the months and years to come as I think about my loved ones.

Thank you, also, for being so kind and receptive from the time I contacted you last August. You answered all my questions. During the reading, you were warm and personal. You struck both my husband and me as a really kind person.

I'm so grateful I could have one of your last private readings for the foreseeable future. I wish you all the best with your next book and will keep track of your journey on your website.

I feel blessed to have had our paths crossed; I will never forget it!

Laura M.
April 22, 2017

If you'd like more information about Anthony's seminars, speaking engagements, retreats, or to schedule a group or private session, please send an inquiry to, neveraloneretreats@gmail.com.

www.anthonyquinata.com

Made in the USA
Coppell, TX
02 August 2024

35516838R10090